MEAT DISHES

Edited by Norma MacMillan and Wendy James
Home economist Gilly Cubitt

ORBIS PUBLISHING London

Introduction

There are lots of new ideas for meat cookery in this book, for family suppers, quick snacks, Sunday lunches and dinner parties.

Both imperial and metric measures are given for each recipe; you should follow only one set of measures as they are not direct conversions. All spoon measures are level unless otherwise stated. Pastry quantities are based on the amount of flour used. Dried herbs may be substituted for fresh herbs; use one-third of the quantity.

Photographs were supplied by Editions Atlas, Editions Atlas/Masson, Editions Atlas/Zadora, Archivio IGDA, Lavinia Press Agency, Orbis GmbH

The material in this book has previously appeared in *The Complete Cook*

First published 1981 in Great Britain by Orbis Publishing Limited, 20–22 Bedfordbury, London WC2

ISBN 0-85613-373-6
Printed in Singapore

Contents

Beef pot roast

Overall timing 3 hours plus marination

Freezing Suitable: reheat, in sauce, in 400°F (200°C) Gas 6 oven for 1 hour

To serve 8–10

4 lb	Braising beef	1.8 kg
	Salt and pepper	
6 oz	Pork fat with rind	175 g
1	Large onion	1
3	Carrots	3
3	Stalks of celery	3
1	Garlic clove	1
	Sprigs of parsley	
2	Bay leaves	2
	Sprigs of thyme	
$\frac{1}{2}$ pint	Red or white wine	300 ml
1 oz	Butter	25 g
2 tbsp	Oil	2x15 ml
1	Pig's trotter	1
4 fl oz	Water	120 ml
1 tbsp	Tomato purée	15 ml

Season the beef. Slice the pork fat. Wrap the fat around the beef and secure with string. Peel and chop the onion and carrots. Trim and chop the celery. Peel and crush the garlic. Tie the parsley, bay leaves and thyme together with string (or use a bouquet garni).

Put the beef in a bowl and add the prepared vegetables, herbs, wine and seasoning. Marinate overnight.

The next day, drain the beef, reserving the marinade. Pat the beef dry with kitchen paper. Melt the butter with the oil in a flameproof casserole and brown the beef on all sides.

Split the trotter and add to the casserole with the marinade, water and tomato purée. Bring to the boil, then cover and simmer for $2\frac{1}{2}$ hours.

Transfer the beef to a warmed serving platter and keep hot. Strain the cooking liquor, discarding the trotter and vegetables, and return to the casserole. Boil the liquor till reduced, then pour into sauceboat. Serve beef with sauce, and carrots and button onions.

Cumin-braised beef

Overall timing 3 hours

Freezing Suitable: reheat from frozen in moderate oven

To serve 6

3 oz	Pork fat	75 g
4 lb	Braising beef	1.8 kg
2	Onions	2
2	Garlic cloves	2
4	Tomatoes	4
4 tbsp	Oil or dripping	4x15 ml
	Salt and pepper	
$\frac{1}{4}$ pint	Dry white wine	150 ml
2 teasp	Paprika	2x5 ml
1 tbsp	Ground cumin	15 ml
$\frac{1}{2}$ pint	Beef stock	300 ml
4 oz	Mushrooms	125 g
1 oz	Butter	25 g

Cut the pork fat into $\frac{1}{2}$ inch (12.5 mm) thick strips. Chill for 20 minutes, then insert into beef with a larding needle. If necessary, tie joint with string to help it keep its shape. Peel and finely chop onions and garlic. Blanch, peel and chop tomatoes.

Heat the oil or dripping in a flameproof casserole and brown the joint on all sides for 10 minutes. Season, pour in the wine and cook over a high heat for 2 minutes. Add onions, garlic, tomatoes, paprika, cumin and half the stock. Cover tightly and cook gently for 2 hours, turning the joint over from time to time.

Slice mushrooms. Melt butter and fry mushrooms for a few minutes. Remove joint from casserole, place on serving plate and keep warm. Add remaining stock and mushrooms to the casserole and bring to the boil. Cover and simmer for 15 minutes. To serve, slice meat and serve sauce separately.

Beef with cucumber sauce

Overall timing $3\frac{1}{4}$ hours

Freezing Suitable: reheat from frozen in moderate oven

To serve 8

2 oz	Pork fat	50 g
$3\frac{1}{2}$ lb	Braising beef	1.6 kg
	Salt and pepper	
2 oz	Dripping	50 g
2	Onions	2
$\frac{1}{2}$ pint	Hot beef stock	300 ml
Sauce		
1 tbsp	Plain flour	15 ml
1 tbsp	Made mustard	15 ml
	Worcestershire sauce	
2 tbsp	Lemon juice	2x15 ml
$\frac{1}{2}$ pint	Carton of soured cream	284 ml
7 oz	Cucumber	200 g
1 tbsp	Dried dill weed	15 ml

Cut fat into strips. Chill for 20 minutes, then insert into joint with a larding needle. Season joint. Melt dripping in a flameproof casserole and brown joint on all sides.

Peel and chop onions, add to casserole and cook till brown. Pour in half stock, cover and cook for 2 hours. Turn joint over from time to time.

Add rest of stock and cook uncovered for a further 30 minutes. Lift out joint on to serving dish, cover and keep warm. Reduce stock by boiling for 5–10 minutes.

Mix flour with a little cold water and stir in. Cook for 5 minutes. Mix mustard, a dash of Worcestershire sauce and the lemon juice into soured cream. Stir into sauce. Chop cucumber and add with dill. Cook gently for 5 minutes. Serve sauce with meat.

Salt beef

Overall timing $3\frac{1}{2}$ hours plus 2 weeks salting

Freezing Not suitable

To serve 8–10

2 lb	Coarse salt	900g
4 oz	Sugar	125 g
1 tbsp	Saltpetre	15 ml
1 oz	Pickling spice	25 g
4	Bay leaves	4
1	Sprig of thyme	1
5 lb	Silverside or brisket of beef	2.3 kg
3	Large onions	3
5	Cloves	5
1	Stalk of celery	1
1 teasp	Black peppercorns	5 ml
1 lb	Medium carrots	450 g
2	Medium turnips	2
1 lb	Leeks	450 g

Put salt, sugar and saltpetre into a large saucepan with pickling spices tied in muslin. Add bay leaves, thyme and 8 pints (4.5 litres) water and heat gently, stirring, till sugar and salt have dissolved. Bring to the boil, then pour into bowl and cool.

Add meat to bowl, making sure that salt solution covers it. Cover with clean tea-towel and leave to soak in cold place for up to 2 weeks. Turn meat occasionally.

To cook, remove from pickle and wash under cold running water. Put into a large saucepan with one onion, peeled and spiked with cloves. Chop celery and add to pan with peppercorns. Cover with cold water and bring to the boil slowly. Skim, reduce heat, cover and simmer for $2\frac{1}{2}$ hours.

Meanwhile, peel and chop carrots and turnips. Peel remaining onions and slice thickly. Chop leeks. Add vegetables to pan, bring back to the boil and simmer for 30 minutes. Use strained cooking liquor to make a sauce.

Boeuf en croûte

Overall timing $1\frac{1}{2}$ hours plus cooling and chilling

Freezing Not suitable

To serve 6

1 lb	Frozen puff pastry	454 g
3 lb	Fillet of beef	1.4 kg
1	Garlic clove	1
1 oz	Softened butter	25 g
	Salt and pepper	
1 teasp	Dried thyme	5 ml
4 oz	Smooth liver pâté	125 g
1	Egg	1

Thaw pastry. Preheat the oven to 425°F (220°C) Gas 7.

Trim meat of all fat, then tie into a neat shape with fine string. Make tiny slits in meat with tip of a sharp knife and insert slivers of peeled garlic. Spread butter over beef, season and sprinkle with half the thyme. Place in roasting tin and roast for 10 minutes. Take meat out of tin, place on a wire rack and leave to cool completely.

Remove string from meat. Roll out dough to a large rectangle just over twice the size of the meat. Place meat on one half of dough rectangle and brush dough edges with water. Spread pâté over top of meat and sprinkle with remaining thyme. Fold dough over to enclose meat and seal edges. Trim round three sides and, if liked, make a hole in the top. Make a funnel from foil and place in hole if liked. Place on dampened baking tray.

Cut decorative shapes out of dough trimmings, dip them into beaten egg and arrange on dough. Glaze all over with egg and chill for 1 hour.

Preheat oven to 425°F (220°C) Gas 7. Bake for 35 minutes till pastry is well risen and golden. Place on a warmed serving dish, garnish with watercress and serve, cut into thick slices.

Roast fillet of beef

Overall timing 1 hour

Freezing Not suitable

To serve 6

4oz	Streaky bacon	125g
$2\frac{1}{4}$ lb	Fillet of beef	1kg
	Salt and pepper	
2	Carrots	2
2	Parsnips	2
2	Onions	2
1	Small cauliflower	1
8oz	Button mushrooms	225g
3oz	Butter	75g
2 teasp	Brown sugar	2x5ml
8oz	Can of French beans	227g
8oz	Frozen peas	225g
2 tbsp	Sherry	2x15ml
8fl oz	Hot beef stock	220ml
1oz	Plain flour	25g

Preheat the oven to 375°F (190°C) Gas 5.

Derind and stretch bacon. Season beef, wrap with bacon, then roll and tie with string into neat shape. Put beef in roasting tin and roast for 40 minutes.

Meanwhile, peel carrots, parsnips and onions. Cut carrots and parsnips into sticks, onions into quarters. Break cauliflower into florets. Place each vegetable on a piece of foil. Divide 2oz (50g) butter between vegetables and season. Sprinkle sugar over carrots and parsnips; parsley over cauliflower and mushrooms. Seal into parcels. Cook in boiling water for 15 minutes. Drain beans and wrap in foil. Wrap peas in foil. Add to pan and cook for 15 minutes.

Remove beef from tin and keep warm. Pour off fat. Add sherry to tin and stir over heat to dissolve meat glaze. Pour in stock. Mix remaining butter to paste with flour and add to tin, stirring till thickened. Season.

Discard string and bacon from beef and slice. Arrange vegetables round meat, pouring juices from foil over.

Spicy meatballs

Overall timing 30 minutes

Freezing Not suitable

To serve 4–6		
1	Small onion	1
1	Garlic clove	1
$1\frac{1}{2}$ lb	Lean minced beef	700 g
1	Egg	1
1 oz	Fresh white breadcrumbs	25 g
	Salt and pepper	
$\frac{1}{2}$ teasp	Ground allspice	2.5 ml
	Oil for frying	

Peel and finely chop the onion; peel and crush the garlic. Put with rest of ingredients (except for the oil) into a bowl and mix well together. Shape mixture into walnut-sized balls.

Fry the meatballs in shallow oil for about 15 minutes, turning once. Arrange on a warmed serving plate and serve with rice or pasta, and a tomato sauce or gravy.

French beef stew

Overall timing $4\frac{1}{2}$ hours

Freezing Suitable: cook for only $2\frac{1}{2}$ hours, and add pork fat, rind and olives after reheating

To serve 8

3	Large onions	3
12 oz	Carrots	350 g
	Rind of 1 orange	
$3\frac{1}{4}$ lb	Chuck steak	1.5 kg
7 oz	Pork fat with rind	200 g
5	Garlic cloves	5
1	Bouquet garni	1
6 tbsp	Tomato purée	6x15 ml
2 tbsp	Oil	2x15 ml
	Salt and pepper	
1	Calf's foot	1
25 fl oz	Bottle of red wine	700 ml
4 oz	Stoned green olives	125 g

Peel onions and cut into thick rings. Peel and thickly slice carrots. Shred orange rind into matchstick strips. Cut meat into large cubes. Cut rind from pork fat. Peel and crush garlic.

Place pork rind, onions, carrots, garlic, bouquet garni, tomato purée, orange rind, oil and seasoning into flameproof casserole. Chop calf's foot in two and add with meat and wine to casserole. Bring to the boil, then cover and simmer for about $3\frac{1}{2}$ hours.

Cut pork fat into thin strips and place in a pan of cold water with olives. Bring to the boil and drain. Add to the casserole and cook for a further 30 minutes.

Lift out bouquet garni and calf's foot and discard. Lift out meat and vegetables and place in a warmed serving dish. Skim sauce and boil over a high heat to reduce it a little. Pour sauce over meat and serve immediately.

Hungarian beef

Overall timing $2\frac{1}{2}$ hours

Freezing Suitable: reheat in 325°F (170°C) Gas 3 oven for 20 minutes, then add vegetables

To serve 4		
$1\frac{1}{2}$ lb	Braising steak	700g
2oz	Lard	50g
2	Onions	2
1 tbsp	Paprika	15ml
$\frac{1}{2}$ teasp	Caraway seeds	2.5ml
$\frac{3}{4}$ pint	Beef stock	400ml
	Salt and pepper	
2	Green peppers	2
8oz	Tomatoes	225g
1lb	Potatoes	450g

Preheat the oven to 325°F (170°C) Gas 3.

Cut steak into four equal-size pieces. Melt half the lard in a flameproof casserole, add the steaks and brown quickly on both sides. Remove from casserole and reserve.

Peel and chop the onions. Add remaining lard to casserole and fry onions gently for about 10 minutes till golden, stirring frequently. Remove casserole from the heat and stir in the paprika, mixing well. Add the caraway seeds, one-third of the stock, the steak and seasoning. Cover and cook in the oven for $1\frac{1}{2}$ hours.

Meanwhile, deseed and slice peppers. Blanch, peel and chop tomatoes. Peel and thinly slice potatoes. Remove casserole from oven and stir in remaining stock, peppers, tomatoes and potatoes. Cover and cook for a further 30 minutes till potatoes are tender. Taste and adjust seasoning.

Lift out meat and place in individual deep serving plates. Spoon vegetables and sauce over.

Goulash

Overall timing $2\frac{1}{4}$ hours

Freezing Suitable

To serve 6

2lb	Stewing beef	900g
2oz	Pork dripping	50g
8oz	Onions	225g
2	Garlic cloves	2
1 tbsp	Plain flour	15ml
1 pint	Beef stock	560ml
$\frac{1}{2}$ teasp	Dried marjoram	2.5ml
$\frac{1}{2}$ teasp	Caraway seed	2.5ml
	Brown sugar	
2 teasp	Paprika	2x5ml
	Salt and pepper	

Cube beef. Heat dripping in a large saucepan or flameproof casserole. Add beef and fry till brown on all sides. Peel and chop onions and garlic. Add to pan and cook till transparent.

Sprinkle in flour and stir into mixture. Add stock, marjoram, caraway seed, a pinch of sugar, paprika and seasoning. Cover tightly and cook gently for $1\frac{3}{4}$–2 hours.

Beef ragoût

Overall timing 2 hours

Freezing Suitable

To serve 4–6		
$1\frac{3}{4}$ lb	Chuck steak	750g
3oz	Piece of streaky bacon	75g
12oz	Onions	350g
2	Tomatoes	2
1 tbsp	Tomato purée	15ml
	Salt and pepper	
2 tbsp	Plain flour	2x15ml
$\frac{1}{4}$ pint	Red wine	150ml
$\frac{1}{2}$ pint	Hot beef stock	300ml
1	Bay leaf	1
4oz	Button mushrooms	125g
1	Green pepper	1
1	Red pepper	1
2 tbsp	Chopped parsley	2x15ml

Cube beef and bacon. Peel and chop onions. Cook bacon in saucepan till fat runs. Add beef and brown all over. Add onions and cook for 3 minutes.

Blanch, peel and chop tomatoes. Stir into pan with tomato purée and seasoning. Sprinkle over flour, stir in well and cook for 3 minutes. Add wine, stock and bay leaf. Cover and simmer for 50 minutes.

Halve mushrooms. Deseed peppers and cut into strips. Add both to pan with parsley and cook for 25 minutes more.

Meat loaf

Overall timing $1\frac{3}{4}$ hours

Freezing Not suitable

To serve 6		
4oz	Sliced bread	125g
1	Onion	1
$1\frac{1}{2}$ lb	Minced beef	700g
2 tbsp	Tomato purée	2x15ml
2	Eggs	2
1 tbsp	Chopped parsley	15ml
	Salt and pepper	
$\frac{1}{2}$ oz	Butter	15g
14oz	Can of tomatoes	397g
1 teasp	Sugar	5ml
	Sprigs of parsley	

Preheat the oven to 350°F (180°C) Gas 4.

Remove crusts from bread and dice. Peel and finely chop onion. Mix with bread, beef, tomato purée, eggs, parsley and seasoning. Spoon into greased 2 pint (1.1 litre) loaf tin. Smooth top, dot with butter and bake for $1\frac{1}{2}$ hours.

Meanwhile, push tomatoes and juice through a sieve into a saucepan. Add sugar and seasoning. Cook till reduced and thick.

Remove meatloaf from oven and cool for 5 minutes. Turn out on to a warmed serving plate. Cut into fairly thick slices and garnish with parsley. Serve with tomato sauce.

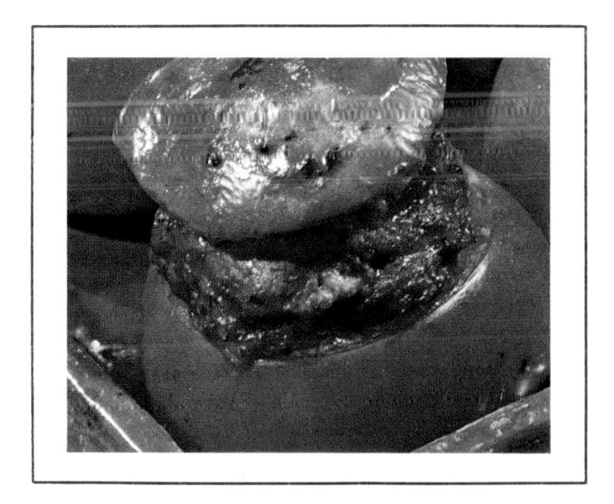

Beefy tomatoes

Overall timing 45 minutes

Freezing Not suitable

To serve 6		
6	Large tomatoes	6
1	Large onion	1
8 oz	Corned beef	225 g
8 oz	Sausagemeat	225 g
2 tbsp	Chopped parsley	2x15 ml
1	Egg	1
¼ teasp	Ground allspice	1.25 ml
	Salt and pepper	
	Oil	

Preheat the oven to 425°F (220°C) Gas 7.

Cut tops off tomatoes and reserve. Scoop out most of the flesh and place it in a bowl. Peel and finely chop onion. Add to bowl with the corned beef, sausagemeat and chopped parsley. Mash well. Beat in the egg, allspice and seasoning and mix well.

Stuff tomatoes with beef mixture and put the reserved "lids" on top. Place on a baking tray and sprinkle with oil. Bake for 20 minutes. Serve with crusty bread.

Nutty beefburgers

Overall timing 45 minutes

Freezing Not suitable

To serve 4		
4 oz	Hazelnuts	125 g
1 oz	Butter	25 g
1	Large onion	1
1 lb	Lean minced beef	450 g
2 tbsp	Capers	2x15 ml
	Grated rind of 1 lemon	
¼ teasp	Paprika	1.25 ml
½ teasp	Powdered mustard	2.5 ml
	Salt and pepper	
4	Egg yolks	4

Preheat the oven to 375°F (190°C) Gas 5.

Chop nuts. Melt butter in a frying pan and cook nuts till golden. Peel onion. Cut four equal rings and reserve. Finely chop remainder and mix with nuts, beef, half the capers, the lemon rind, paprika, mustard and seasoning.

Divide mixture into four portions. Shape into balls, place on a baking tray and flatten slightly making a well in centre of each. Bake for 25 minutes.

Place each burger on a lettuce leaf on serving plate. Press an onion ring into each well, then carefully place a raw egg yolk in each ring and garnish with remaining capers. If liked, bake for a further 10 minutes to cook egg yolk.

Steak in cream sauce

Overall timing 15 minutes

Freezing Not suitable

To serve 4–6

1 lb	Fillet steak	450 g
3 oz	Butter	75 g
	Sprig of rosemary	
	Salt and pepper	
1 teasp	French mustard	5 ml
1 teasp	Worcestershire sauce	5 ml
$\frac{1}{4}$ pint	Carton of single cream	150 ml
2 tbsp	Grand Marnier	2x15 ml

Cut steak into $\frac{1}{4}$ inch (6 mm) slices with a sharp knife. Melt the butter in a frying pan, add sprig of rosemary and seasoning and fry steak slices, two at a time, over a high heat for 2–3 minutes on each side. As steaks are cooked, remove from pan and keep hot.

Add mustard and Worcestershire sauce to the pan, then stir in the cream. Mix well, then return steaks to the pan. Cook for 1 minute over gentle heat, then turn steaks over.

Heat the liqueur in a ladle, pour over the steaks and set alight. Cover and turn off the heat. Wait for 2 minutes, then serve.

Steak with mushrooms

Overall timing 30 minutes

Freezing Not suitable

To serve 4

12 oz	Button mushrooms	350 g
2 oz	Butter	50 g
2 tbsp	Oil	2x15 ml
4	Porterhouse steaks	4
4 fl oz	Dry white wine	120 ml
$\frac{1}{2}$ teasp	Dried thyme	2.5 ml
$\frac{1}{4}$ teasp	Garlic salt	1.25 ml
	Grated nutmeg	
	Pepper	

Slice the mushrooms. Melt the butter in a frying pan and fry the mushrooms for 5 minutes till golden. Remove from the pan and reserve.

Add the oil to the pan and heat till very hot. Put the steaks in the pan and fry for 2 minutes on each side to seal them. Reduce the heat and continue frying for 2–4 minutes on each side according to taste. Arrange the steaks on a warmed serving dish and keep hot.

Pour off excess fat from the pan. Add the wine, thyme and garlic salt and bring to the boil, stirring in the sediment from the bottom of the pan. Boil till reduced by half, then add the mushrooms with nutmeg and pepper to taste. Cook till the mushrooms are heated through.

Arrange the mushrooms around the steaks and pour the pan juices over.

Neapolitan beef

Overall timing $2\frac{1}{2}$ hours

Freezing Not suitable

To serve 4

2 oz	Back bacon	50 g
2 oz	Belly pork fat	50 g
1 tbsp	Chopped parsley	15 ml
1 tbsp	Seedless raisins	15 ml
	Salt and pepper	
1 lb	Top rump of beef	450 g
1	Onion	1
1	Garlic clove	1
2 tbsp	Oil	2x15 ml
14 oz	Can of tomatoes	397 g
$\frac{1}{2}$ pint	Beef stock	300 ml
12 oz	Rigatoni	350 g
2 tbsp	Grated Parmesan cheese	2x15 ml

Chop or finely mince bacon and pork fat and mix with parsley to form a smooth paste. Work in raisins and seasoning. With a larding needle, make several deep holes in meat and firmly stuff paste into them. Tie meat into a neat roll with string.

Peel and finely chop onion. Peel and crush garlic. Heat oil in flameproof casserole, add onion and garlic and fry till transparent. Add the meat roll and fry, turning frequently, to seal. Press tomatoes and their juice through a sieve and add to casserole with the stock and seasoning. Mix well, cover and simmer for $1\frac{1}{2}$ hours or till tender.

Meanwhile, cook rigatoni in boiling salted water till tender. Drain and keep hot.

Lift meat out of casserole, remove string and slice. Arrange on a warmed serving dish and arrange rigatoni round meat. Taste sauce and adjust seasoning. Spoon sauce over meat and rigatoni. Sprinkle with Parmesan. Serve immediately.

Tortellini beef pie

Overall timing $1\frac{3}{4}$ hours

Freezing Suitable: bake for only 30 minutes; reheat from frozen in oven for 30 minutes, then cover and bake for 20 minutes more

To serve 8

1	Onion	1
1	Carrot	1
1	Stalk of celery	1
4oz	Streaky bacon	125g
1oz	Butter	25g
1lb	Minced beef	450g
3fl oz	Red wine	90ml
$1\frac{1}{4}$ pints	Beef stock	700ml
1 tbsp	Tomato purée	15ml
	Salt and pepper	
$\frac{1}{4}$ teasp	Grated nutmeg	1.25ml
8oz	Tortellini	225g
1lb	Shortcrust pastry	450g
4 tbsp	Grated Parmesan cheese	4x15ml
$\frac{1}{2}$ pint	White sauce	300ml
1	Egg yolk	1

Peel and finely chop onion and carrot. Chop celery. Derind and dice bacon. Melt butter in a saucepan, add beef, bacon and vegetables and fry for 5 minutes. Add wine, $\frac{1}{4}$ pint (150ml) stock, tomato purée, seasoning and nutmeg and simmer for 15 minutes.

Meanwhile, cook tortellini in remaining boiling stock till tender. Drain and cool.

Preheat the oven to 400°F (200°C) Gas 6.

Roll out two-thirds of dough and use to line an $8\frac{1}{2}$ inch (22cm) springform tin. Cover bottom with one-third tortellini, then half meat sauce and Parmesan. Repeat layers, then pour over white sauce and cover with remaining tortellini.

Roll out remaining dough and use to cover pie. Brush with beaten egg yolk. Bake for 1 hour, covering the top lightly with foil halfway through cooking. Serve hot or cold.

Veal

Roast veal in white wine with onions

Overall timing $1\frac{1}{2}$ hours

Freezing Not suitable

To serve 4

2oz	Butter	50g
2	Carrots	2
1	Large onion	1
1	Garlic clove	1
$2\frac{1}{2}$ lb	Fillet of veal	1.1kg
	Salt and pepper	
$\frac{1}{4}$ pint	Dry white wine	150ml
1lb	Button onions	450g
2	Cloves	2
	Chopped parsley	

Preheat the oven to 450°F (230°C) Gas 8.

Grease roasting tin with $\frac{1}{2}$oz (15g) butter. Peel and finely chop carrots and large onion. Peel and crush garlic. Put vegetables into roasting tin. Tie fillet into a neat shape with fine string, place on top of vegetables and spread remaining butter over. Season. Pour wine into tin and roast for 20 minutes to seal the meat.

Meanwhile, blanch and peel button onions and spike two with cloves. Remove meat from the oven. Strain cooking liquor, discarding flavourings. Return liquor and meat to the tin. Reduce the oven temperature to 400°F (200°C) Gas 6. Add button onions to the tin, turning them till coated with the cooking liquor. Return tin to oven and roast for a further 40 minutes till tender, basting meat and onions twice.

Discard string and carve meat into thin slices. Arrange on a warmed serving dish surrounded by the onions (discard cloves). Reduce cooking liquor in tin by fast boiling on top of the stove and spoon over meat. Garnish with chopped parsley and serve.

Roast veal with prunes

Overall timing $1\frac{3}{4}$ hours plus overnight soaking

Freezing Not suitable

To serve 6

8 oz	Plump prunes	225 g
5 tbsp	Brandy	5x15 ml
8 oz	Back bacon rashers	225 g
1 oz	Butter	25 g
$2\frac{1}{2}$ lb	Rolled boned leg of veal	1.1 kg
	Salt and pepper	
1 tbsp	Plain flour	15 ml
$\frac{1}{4}$ pint	Light stock	150 ml

Slit the prunes carefully and remove stones. Put the prunes into a bowl with the brandy and soak overnight.

Next day, preheat the oven to 400°F (200°C) Gas 6.

Derind and halve the bacon rashers. Melt the butter in flameproof casserole and lightly fry the bacon. Remove from the pan and reserve. Coat the veal with seasoned flour. Put the veal into the casserole and brown on all sides. Add any remaining flour and cook for 1 minute. Gradually add the stock and bring to the boil, stirring constantly. Season, cover tightly and cook in the oven for about 1 hour.

Drain the prunes and pour brandy into a saucepan. Heat gently, then pour over the veal and set alight. When the flames have died down, add prunes and bacon to casserole. Season, cover and continue cooking in the oven for 30–40 minutes till the meat is tender.

Remove veal from pan, cut into slices and arrange on a warmed serving dish. Arrange prunes and bacon with the veal and pour the liquor over. Serve immediately with roast potatoes and parsleyed carrots.

Veal cordon bleu

Overall timing 35 minutes plus chilling

Freezing Suitable: cook after thawing

To serve 4		
4x7 oz	Thick veal escalopes	4x200 g
	Salt and pepper	
4	Slices of cooked ham	4
4	Slices of cheese	4
2 tbsp	Plain flour	2x15 ml
2	Eggs	2
3 tbsp	Breadcrumbs	3x15 ml
2 oz	Butter	50 g
2 tbsp	Oil	2x15 ml
1	Lemon	1
1	Tomato	1

Cut a pocket in each escalope. Season inside, then put a slice of ham and a slice of cheese inside each and close with wooden cocktail sticks. Coat first in flour, then in egg and finally in breadcrumbs. Place on baking tray and chill for 30 minutes, if possible.

Heat butter and oil in a frying pan. Cook escalopes, two at a time, for 6–8 minutes on each side. Keep them warm on the serving dish then, when all are cooked, remove cocktail sticks, garnish with lemon and tomato and serve.

Veal with paprika sauce

Overall timing 40 minutes

Freezing Not suitable

To serve 4		
1 lb	Onions	450 g
3 tbsp	Oil	3x15 ml
1 tbsp	Paprika	15 ml
14 oz	Can of tomatoes	397 g
2 tbsp	Tomato purée	2x15 ml
1 teasp	Sugar	5 ml
	Salt and pepper	
1	Green pepper	1
4	Veal escalopes	4
4 tbsp	Plain flour	4x15 ml
2 oz	Butter	50 g
6 tbsp	Red wine	6x15 ml
1 tbsp	Chopped parsley	15 ml

Peel and thinly slice onions. Heat oil in saucepan and fry onions till golden. Add paprika and fry for 1 minute. Stir in tomatoes and juice, tomato purée, sugar and seasoning. Simmer for 15 minutes.

Meanwhile, deseed and slice pepper. Coat veal with seasoned flour. Melt butter in frying pan and fry veal for 5–8 minutes on each side. Remove from pan and keep hot. Add pepper to pan and fry for 3 minutes. Stir in wine to dissolve sediment, then add to tomato mixture with parsley. Pour into serving dish and arrange veal on top.

Poached veal puffs

Overall timing 1 hour plus chilling

Freezing Not suitable

To serve 4		
1½ lb	Hot mashed potato	700g
4 tbsp	Plain flour	4x15ml
2oz	Butter	50g
4tbsp	Grated Parmesan cheese	4x15ml
	Salt and pepper	
12oz	Cooked veal	350ml
4oz	Cream cheese	125g
¼ teasp	Tabasco	1.25ml
¼ pint	Carton of single cream	150ml
2 teasp	Paprika	2x5ml

Beat potato with flour, butter, Parmesan and seasoning. Chill for 2–3 hours till firm.

Mince veal and beat into cream cheese with Tabasco and seasoning.

Divide potato into 12 portions. Shape into balls with floured hands, make a hole in centre, fill with veal mixture, then seal with potato. Poach in boiling salted water for about 10 minutes, till puffs float to surface. Drain well and arrange on warmed serving dish.

Warm cream and season. Pour over puffs and sprinkle with paprika.

Veal with peppercorns

Overall timing 30 minutes

Freezing Not suitable

To serve 4		
4	Veal escalopes	4
	Salt and pepper	
3 tbsp	Plain flour	3x15ml
2oz	Butter	50g
1 tbsp	Oil	15ml
2 tbsp	Brined green peppercorns	2x15ml
¼ pint	Dry white wine	150ml
2 tbsp	Brandy	2x15ml
¼ pint	Carton of double cream	150ml

Coat veal with seasoned flour. Heat butter and oil in a frying pan and brown veal on both sides. Remove from pan and keep hot.

Crush drained peppercorns lightly with the back of a spoon. Add to pan with wine and heat gently, scraping sediment from bottom of pan. Bring to the boil and boil rapidly till reduced by half.

Return veal to pan. Warm brandy, pour over veal and set alight. Stir in cream when flames have died down, cover and cook gently for 5 minutes.

Arrange veal escalopes on a warmed serving dish. Taste sauce and adjust seasoning. Pour round the veal and serve immediately with sauté potatoes.

Piquant veal

Overall timing 25 minutes

Freezing Not suitable

To serve 6

2	Anchovy fillets	2
2oz	Chicken livers	50g
1	Garlic clove	1
1	Lemon	1
2oz	Cooked ham	50g
3	Sage leaves	3
1 tbsp	Capers	15ml
6	Veal escalopes	6
2 tbsp	Olive oil	2x15ml
	Salt and pepper	

Chop anchovies and chicken livers. Peel and crush garlic. Grate rind of lemon and squeeze out juice. Finely chop ham and sage. Mix together anchovies, livers, garlic, lemon rind and juice, ham, sage and capers.

Place escalopes between sheets of damp greaseproof and flatten with a meat bat or rolling-pin. Heat the oil in a frying pan, add veal and fry for 3–5 minutes on each side.

Add anchovy mixture and seasoning. Cook over low heat for 3–5 minutes, shaking pan occasionally to prevent sticking. Arrange on a warmed serving dish and garnish with sage leaves. Serve with boiled new potatoes and a green salad.

Veal escalopes with cherries

Overall timing 25 minutes

Freezing Not suitable

To serve 4

4x7oz	Veal escalopes	4x200g
	Salt and pepper	
2oz	Butter	50g
1 tbsp	Oil	15ml
2 tbsp	Plain flour	2x15ml
4 tbsp	Red wine	4x15ml
4 tbsp	Single cream	4x15ml
9oz	Can of cherries	250g
	Parsley	

Season escalopes. Heat butter and oil in frying pan, add veal and cook for $\frac{1}{2}$ minute on each side, then 3 minutes on each side. Remove from pan and keep warm.

Stir flour into the pan juices, then mix in the wine, cream and seasoning.

Heat cherries in their juice, then drain, adding a little of the juice to the sauce in the pan. Stir well to combine.

Arrange escalopes on a warmed plate with the cherries around them. Pour the sauce over and garnish with parsley.

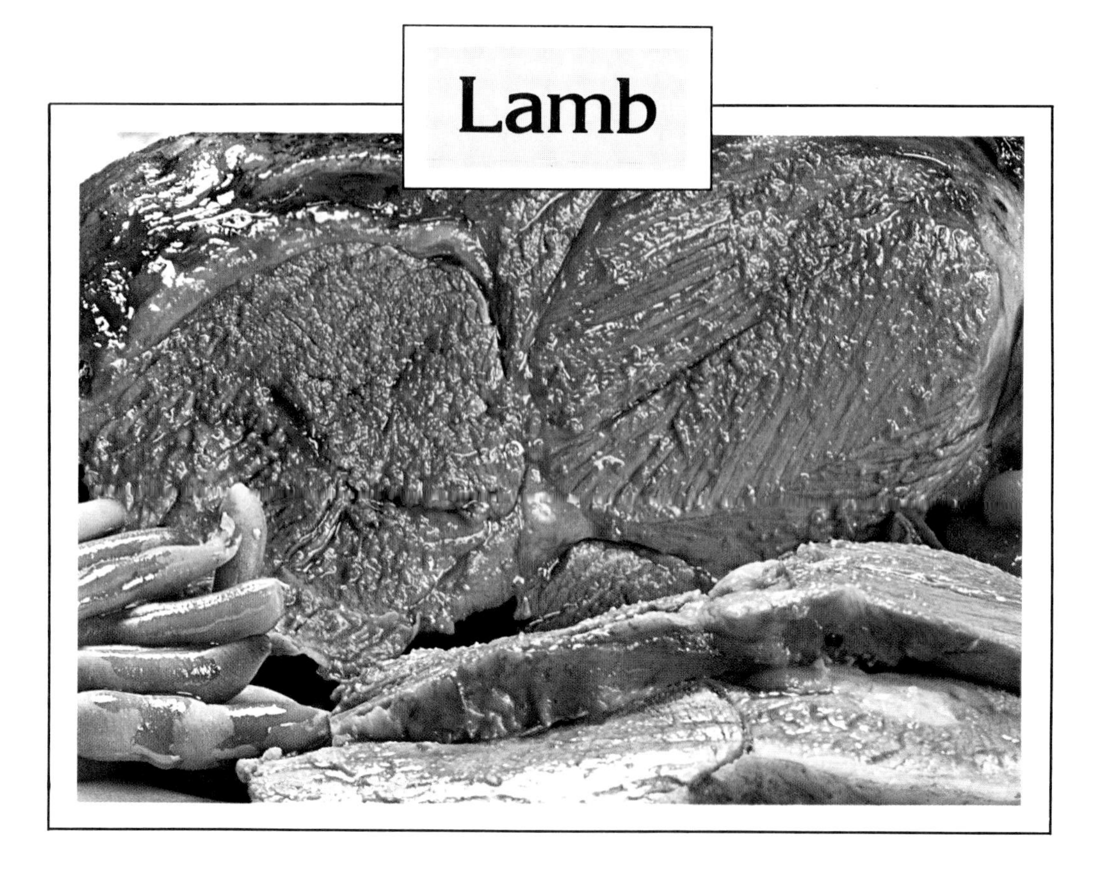

Roast lamb with garlic

Overall timing 2 hours

Freezing Not suitable

To serve 6

2–3	Garlic cloves	2–3
$3\frac{1}{2}$ lb	Leg of lamb	1.6 kg
1 oz	Butter or dripping	25 g
	Salt and pepper	

Preheat the oven to 350°F (180°C) Gas 4.

Peel the garlic cloves and cut each into thin slivers. Place lamb in roasting tin with the thickest fat uppermost. Using a sharp, thin bladed knife, make incisions about 1 inch (2.5 cm) deep in the meat. Insert a sliver of garlic into each incision, pressing it down so it is level with the surface of the meat.

Spread the softened butter or dripping over the lamb and season well. Roast for $1\frac{3}{4}$ hours or until the juices run clear when a skewer is inserted into the thickest part of the meat.

Transfer meat to warmed serving plate and make the gravy in the usual way. Serve with green beans and tomatoes.

Italian-style roast lamb

Overall timing $1\frac{1}{2}$ hours

Freezing Not suitable

To serve 4

2 lb	Chump end of loin of lamb	900 g
	Sprigs of rosemary	
2 lb	Potatoes	900 g
2 tbsp	Oil	2x15 ml
3 oz	Butter	75 g
1	Garlic clove	1
	Salt and pepper	

Preheat the oven to 350°F (180°C) Gas 4.

Slash through the chops, leaving the loin joined at the bottom. Place sprigs of rosemary in the slashes. Peel potatoes and cut into chunks.

Heat oil and butter in roasting tin. Add the meat and arrange potatoes around it. Peel and crush garlic and add to the lamb and potatoes with salt and pepper. Roast for 45 minutes–1 hour, basting occasionally and turning potatoes halfway through cooking. Serve with a mixed salad or a seasonal green vegetable and gravy.

Lamb with potatoes and onions

Overall timing $2\frac{1}{2}$ hours

Freezing Not suitable

To serve 8

$4\frac{1}{2}$ lb	Leg of lamb	2kg
4oz	Butter	125g
	Salt and pepper	
1lb	Onions	450g
2lb	Potatoes	900g
$\frac{3}{4}$ pint	Stock	400ml
	Sprigs of rosemary	
	Bouquet garni	

Preheat the oven to 350°F (180°C) Gas 4.

Place meat in roasting tin, spread with half the butter and season. Roast for $1\frac{1}{4}$ hours.

Peel and slice the onions. Peel and quarter potatoes. Melt remaining butter in frying pan, add onions and potatoes and fry till golden brown. Add stock, rosemary, bouquet garni and seasoning and cook for 5 minutes, stirring occasionally.

Arrange potato mixture around meat and roast for a further 45 minutes till meat is tender.

Remove bouquet garni. Place lamb on warmed serving dish and surround with potato mixture. Serve with green vegetables.

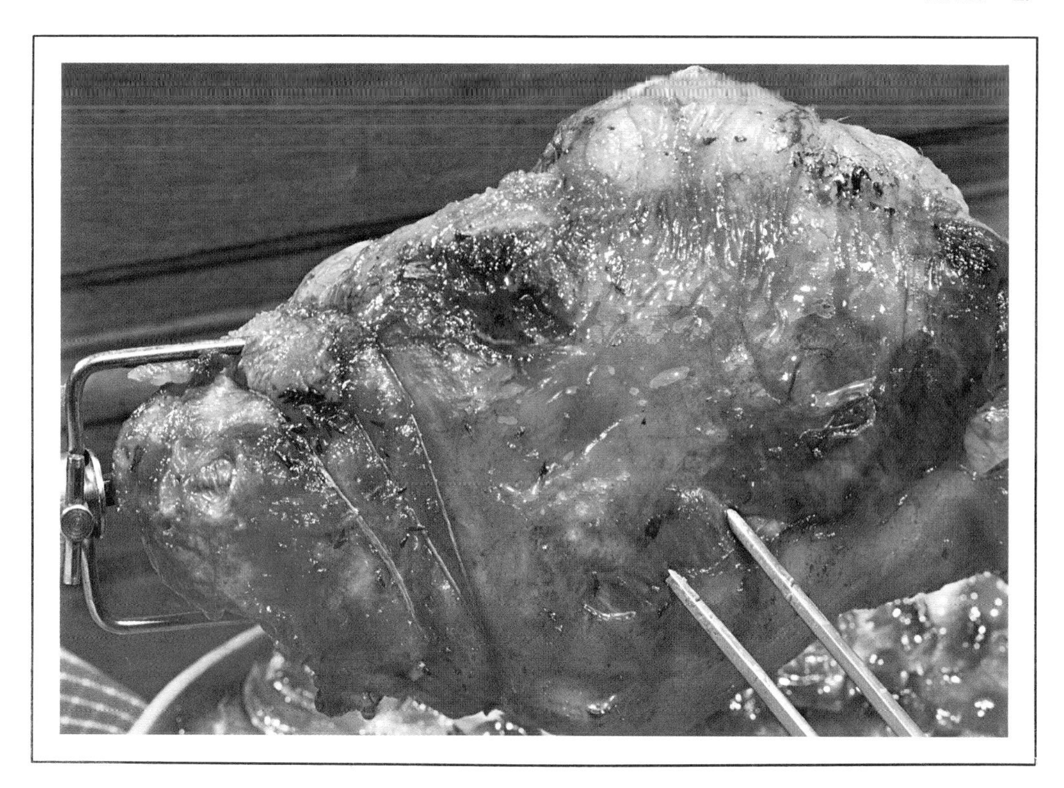

Brittany roast lamb

Overall timing 2½ hours

Freezing Not suitable

To serve 6

3	Garlic cloves	3
4 lb	Leg of lamb	1.8 kg
4 oz	Butter	125 g
	Salt and pepper	
3 lb	Waxy potatoes	1.4 kg
1 teasp	Dried thyme	5 ml

Preheat the oven to 375°F (190°C) Gas 5.

Peel the garlic cloves and slice very thinly. Make incisions through the skin of the lamb and push the garlic into them. Rub half the butter over the lamb and season well.

Grease ovenproof dish with 1 oz (25 g) butter. Peel potatoes and cut into slices about ⅛ inch (3 mm) thick. Arrange half over bottom of dish. Sprinkle with half the thyme and seasoning and dot with half the remaining butter. Repeat layer.

Place dish centrally on shelf below centre of the oven. Place the lamb directly on to the oven shelf above the potatoes so the juices will run on to the potatoes. Roast for 1¾–2 hours till the juices are only slightly pink when thickest part of meat is pierced with a fine skewer.

Place the lamb on a warmed serving dish and carve. Serve the potatoes from the ovenproof dish with a separate dish of cauliflower and whole green beans.

Stuffed breast of lamb

Overall timing $2\frac{1}{2}$ hours

Freezing Not suitable

To serve 8

1 or 2	Boned breasts of lamb	1 or 2
2lb	Potatoes	900g
$1\frac{1}{2}$ lb	Small carrots	700g
4	Turnips	4
2	Stalks of celery	2
4	Leeks	4
1	Onion	1
4	Cloves	4
2oz	Butter	50g
1 pint	Stock	560ml
	Bouquet garni	
Stuffing		
3	Lambs' kidneys	3
8oz	Streaky bacon	225g
8oz	Sausagemeat	225g
$\frac{1}{2}$ teasp	Ground allspice	2.5ml
3 tbsp	Chopped parsley	3x15ml
1 teasp	Dried marjoram	5ml
1	Egg	1
	Salt and pepper	

Preheat the oven to 325°F (170°C) Gas 3.

Prepare and finely chop kidneys. Derind and chop bacon. Mix all stuffing ingredients.

Cut a deep pocket in lamb and fill with stuffing. Sew up opening. If using two breasts, place together with skin side out and sew around sides.

Peel potatoes and carrots. Peel and halve turnips. Chop celery and leeks. Peel onion and spike with cloves. Melt butter in flameproof casserole, add meat and brown all over. Remove. Add vegetables and fry for 2 minutes. Return meat and add stock, bouquet garni and salt. Cover and cook in oven for 2 hours.

Slice meat. Arrange vegetables around meat, discarding onion. Boil stock till reduced by half. Strain over vegetables.

Shoulder of lamb with turnips

Overall timing 2 hours

Freezing Not suitable

To serve 6

3 lb	Boned shoulder of lamb	1.4 kg
	Salt and pepper	
1	Carrot	1
1	Onion	1
3 oz	Butter	75 g
	Bouquet garni	
$\frac{1}{4}$ pint	Stock	150 ml
2 lb	Turnips	900 g
8 oz	Buttons onions	225 g

Preheat the oven to 350°F (180°C) Gas 4.

Season the lamb inside and out. Roll up and tie firmly with string into a neat shape. Peel and thinly slice carrot and onion.

Melt the butter in flameproof casserole, add onion and carrot and fry till golden. Add lamb and brown on all sides. Season and add bouquet garni and stock. Cover and cook in centre of oven for 1 hour.

Peel turnips and button onions. Place in a saucepan of cold salted water and bring to the boil. Drain and dry on kitchen paper. Arrange turnips and onions around the meat and adjust seasoning. Return to oven and cook for a further 45 minutes.

Remove bouquet garni and string. Transfer lamb to warmed serving plate and surround with turnips and onions.

Moroccan-style breast of lamb

Overall timing 1½ hours

Freezing Not suitable

To serve 6

2½ lb	Chopped breast of lamb or riblets	1.1 kg
2 oz	Butter	50 g
	Salt and pepper	
4 fl oz	White wine vinegar	120 ml
3 fl oz	Water	90 ml
2 tbsp	Caster sugar	2x15 ml
2 tbsp	Chopped mint	2x15 ml

Preheat the oven to 350°F (180°C) Gas 4.

Place lamb in roasting tin. Melt butter in saucepan and pour over lamb. Season. Cook in oven for 35 minutes, then turn pieces over and cook for another 35 minutes or until tender. Baste frequently.

Put vinegar, water and sugar in a saucepan. Bring to the boil, stirring. Remove from heat, stir in mint and pour into warmed sauce boat.

Place lamb on a warmed serving dish and spoon juices over. Serve with mint sauce and rice.

Casseroled lamb

Overall timing 2 hours

Freezing Not suitable

To serve 6

1	Carrot	1
1	Onion	1
1	Stalk of celery	1
4	Spring onions	4
3 oz	Streaky bacon	75 g
1	Garlic clove	1
2 tbsp	Oil	2x15 ml
3 tbsp	Chopped parsley	3x15 ml
$2\frac{1}{2}$ lb	Boned shoulder of lamb	1.1 kg
2 oz	Mushrooms	50 g
$\frac{1}{2}$ pint	Dry cider	300 ml
$\frac{1}{4}$ pint	Stock	150 ml
	Salt and pepper	
1 lb	Potatoes	450 g

Peel and chop carrot and onion. Trim and chop celery and spring onions. Derind and chop bacon. Peel and crush garlic. Heat oil in flameproof casserole, add bacon, onion, spring onions, celery, carrot, garlic and parsley and fry till lightly browned.

Tie meat into shape, if necessary, add to casserole and brown on all sides over high heat. Chop mushrooms. Add to casserole with cider, stock and seasoning. Cover and cook for 1 hour over low heat.

Meanwhile, peel and quarter potatoes. Add to casserole and cook, covered, for a further 30 minutes. Taste and adjust seasoning then serve with broccoli.

Lamb steaks with beans

Overall timing 45 minutes

Freezing Not suitable

To serve 4

$1\frac{1}{2}$ lb	Green beans	700 g
2 oz	Butter	50 g
	Salt and pepper	
4 fl oz	Meat stock	120 ml
5 tbsp	Oil	5x15 ml
2	Slices of white bread	2
$\frac{1}{4}$ teasp	Garlic salt	1.25 ml
4	Lamb steaks	4
1 teasp	Mustard seed	5 ml
2 tbsp	Chopped parsley	2x15 ml
2	Tomatoes	2
	Sprigs of parsley	

Top and tail beans and remove strings. Break or cut into short lengths. Melt the butter in a saucepan. Add the beans and cook for a few minutes. Season with salt and pour in the stock. Cook for 10–15 minutes till just tender.

Meanwhile, heat half the oil in a frying pan. Halve the slices of bread and lightly brown them on both sides in the oil. Remove from pan and keep warm.

Add rest of oil to pan and heat. Sprinkle garlic salt over the lamb steaks. Cook the steaks for 5 minutes on each side. Sprinkle with salt, then with pepper mixed with ground mustard seed.

Mix chopped parsley into beans and spread over bottom of warmed serving dish. Put the lamb steaks on the bread and place on top of the beans. Garnish with tomatoes, cut into eighths, and a few parsley sprigs.

Tarragon chops

Overall timing 25 minutes plus chilling

Freezing Not suitable

To serve 4

4oz	Softened butter	125g
1 tbsp	Chopped fresh tarragon	15ml
1 tbsp	Dry white wine	15ml
	Salt and pepper	
4	Double loin lamb chops	4
	Tarragon leaves	

Mash the butter in a bowl with the tarragon, wine and seasoning till evenly mixed. Put half into a small serving dish and chill for 1 hour till firm.

Preheat the grill. Curl the thin tail pieces of the chops in next to the eye to make a neat shape and secure with skewers. Arrange on the grill pan. Spread half the soft tarragon butter over the chops and grill for 6–7 minutes.

Turn the chops with tongs and spread with the remaining soft tarragon butter. Grill for a further 5–7 minutes according to taste.

Arrange the chops on a warmed serving dish and pour the juices from the grill pan over. Top each chop with a curl of the chilled tarragon butter and a tarragon leaf. Serve immediately with remaining tarragon butter.

Lamb cutlets with garlic and anchovy

Overall timing 40 minutes

Freezing Not suitable

To serve 4

2lb	Best end of neck lamb cutlets	900g
2	Garlic cloves	2
5 tbsp	Oil	5x15ml
	Salt and pepper	
	Sprigs of rosemary	
2	Anchovy fillets	2
3 tbsp	White wine vinegar	3x15ml

Trim cutlets of all fat. Peel and crush one garlic clove. Heat the oil in a large frying pan. Add the garlic and cutlets. Fry quickly on both sides till golden, then season, reduce heat and cook for a further 10–15 minutes.

Put a few pieces of fresh rosemary, the remaining garlic clove, peeled, and the anchovies in a mortar. Pound with a pestle, gradually mixing in the vinegar. Add garlic mixture to pan and cook till the liquid reduces by half.

Arrange cutlets on warmed serving dish and spoon cooking juices over. Garnish with remaining rosemary sprigs.

Lamb cutlets niçoise

Overall timing 1 hour

Freezing Not suitable

To serve 4

1 lb	Potatoes	450 g
2 oz	Butter	50 g
2 tbsp	Olive oil	2x15 ml
	Salt and pepper	
1 teasp	Dried rosemary	5 ml
1 teasp	Dried thyme	5 ml
1 teasp	Dried sage	5 ml
4	Large lamb cutlets	4
12 oz	Green beans	350 g
2	Large tomatoes	2
1 tbsp	Chopped parsley	15 ml
3 fl oz	Dry white wine	90 ml
1 tbsp	Tomato purée	15 ml
1	Small garlic clove	1

Peel and dice potatoes. Cover with cold water, bring to the boil, then drain. Melt half butter with half oil in a frying pan, add potatoes and fry for 10 minutes till golden on all sides. Season. Remove from pan and keep hot.

Mix rosemary, thyme and sage and sprinkle over cutlets. Heat remaining oil in frying pan, add cutlets and cook for 5–10 minutes on each side till tender.

Meanwhile, trim beans. Cook in boiling salted water for 10 minutes till tender. Drain, toss in remaining butter and season.

Arrange cutlets, potatoes and beans on warmed serving dish. Halve tomatoes and fry in fat left from cutlets. Arrange on serving dish. Garnish with parsley. Keep hot.

Remove excess fat from frying pan. Add wine, tomato purée and peeled and crushed garlic. Bring to the boil and cook for 3 minutes, stirring. Season and serve separately.

Lamb kebabs with prunes

Overall timing 50 minutes

Freezing Not suitable

To serve 4

12	Prunes	12
$\frac{1}{4}$ pint	Red wine	150 ml
1 lb	Lean lamb cut from the leg	450 g
3 tbsp	Oil	3x15 ml
	Salt and pepper	
$\frac{1}{2}$ teasp	Dried thyme	2.5 ml
2	Firm tomatoes	2
1	Medium onion	1
3	Thick rashers of streaky bacon	3

Put the prunes into a saucepan, add the red wine and bring to the boil. Remove from the heat and leave to soak for 30 minutes.

Cut lamb into 12 large cubes. Place in bowl with oil, seasoning and thyme. Cover and leave for 30 minutes.

Meanwhile, quarter the tomatoes. Peel the onion and cut through the root into eight wedges. Derind bacon and cut each rasher into four. Preheat the grill.

Drain the prunes, reserving the wine. Make a slit in each prune and remove the stone. Thread the lamb, prunes, tomatoes, bacon and onion on to four skewers. Brush the kebabs with the lamb marinade and the wine from the prunes, then sprinkle with salt and pepper. Grill for about 15 minutes, turning occasionally, till the lamb is tender. Arrange on a warmed serving dish and serve with boiled rice.

Marinated lamb kebabs

Overall timing 1 hour

Freezing Not suitable

To serve 6

$1\frac{1}{2}$ lb	Boned shoulder of lamb	700g
1lb	Lean veal	450g
1	Large garlic clove	1
4fl oz	Oil	120ml
4 tbsp	Lemon juice	4x15ml
	Cayenne pepper	
	Salt and pepper	
12	Button onions	12
4	Tomatoes	4
1	Aubergine	1
12	Cubes of bread	12
6	Small bay leaves	6
6	Mushrooms	6

Cut lamb and veal into bite-size pieces. Peel and crush the garlic and mix with the oil, lemon juice, a pinch of cayenne pepper and seasoning. Add the meat and marinate for 30 minutes, stirring frequently.

Peel onions. Quarter tomatoes and cut aubergine into pieces. Preheat the grill and line grill pan with foil.

Drain meat, reserving marinade, and thread on to six skewers with bread, onions, bay leaves, tomatoes, aubergine and mushrooms (flute them if liked). Grill kebabs for 15 minutes, turning and basting with marinade frequently. Serve hot.

Minted lamb brochettes

Overall timing 20 minutes plus 2 hours marination

Freezing Not suitable

To serve 4

2lb	Boned shoulder of lamb	900g
1	Garlic clove	1
¼ pint	Red wine	150ml
2 tbsp	Oil	2x15ml
	Salt and pepper	
	Fresh mint	

Cut lamb into 1 inch (2.5cm) cubes. Peel and crush the garlic and mix with the wine, oil and seasoning. Put the meat into the marinade, cover and marinate in the refrigerator for 2 hours.

Preheat the grill and line grill pan with foil.

Drain meat, reserving marinade, and thread on to four skewers. Grill brochettes for 10 minutes, turning and brushing with marinade frequently. Sprinkle with finely chopped fresh mint and serve hot with saffron rice.

Turkish meatballs

Overall timing 50 minutes

Freezing Suitable: coat with egg and cook from frozen

To serve 6

1	Onion	1
2	Garlic cloves	2
1½ lb	Minced lamb	700g
3	Eggs	3
1 teasp	Olive oil	5ml
1 tbsp	Chopped parsley	15ml
1 teasp	Ground coriander	5ml
	Salt and pepper	
¼ pint	Stock	150ml
4 tbsp	Plain flour	4x15ml
2oz	Butter	50g

Peel and finely chop onion. Peel and crush garlic. Mix both with lamb, two eggs, the oil, parsley, coriander and seasoning to a stiff paste. Shape into 1½ inch (4cm) balls with wet hands and arrange in frying pan.

Gently add stock and bring to the boil. Cover and simmer for 20 minutes, shaking pan occasionally to prevent meatballs sticking. Lift out meatballs with a draining spoon and cool.

Beat remaining egg. Coat meatballs in egg, then in flour. Melt butter in another frying pan, add meatballs and fry over a high heat, turning till crisp and brown.

Lamb and spinach stew

Overall timing $1\frac{3}{4}$ hours

Freezing Not suitable

To serve 4–6

$1\frac{1}{2}$ lb	Boned lean lamb	700g
1	Onion	1
2 tbsp	Oil	2x15ml
	Salt and pepper	
$\frac{1}{4}$ teasp	Chilli powder	1.25ml
3 tbsp	Tomato purée	3x15ml
$\frac{1}{2}$ pint	Water	300ml
$1\frac{1}{2}$ lb	Spinach	700g

Cut the lamb into 1 inch (2.5cm) cubes. Peel and chop the onion. Heat the oil in a saucepan, add the lamb and onion and fry, stirring, till browned all over. Add a little salt and the chilli pepper, cover and cook for 3 minutes.

Add the tomato purée and water. Bring to to the boil, cover and simmer for 1 hour till the lamb is tender.

Pick over the spinach. Shred coarsely and add to the pan. Cover and cook for a further 10 minutes. Taste and adjust the seasoning, arrange on a warmed serving dish and serve immediately with boiled rice.

Country lamb casserole

Overall timing $1\frac{1}{4}$ hours

Freezing Not suitable

To serve 4

1	Large onion	1
4oz	Streaky bacon	125g
$1\frac{1}{2}$ lb	Boned shoulder of lamb	700g
2oz	Butter	50g
1lb	Potatoes	450g
$\frac{1}{4}$ pint	Red wine	150ml
	Salt and pepper	
12	Button onions	12

Peel and slice large onion. Derind and dice bacon. Cut lamb into large pieces. Melt half butter in a flameproof casserole and fry onion till golden. Add bacon and lamb and brown on all sides.

Peel and quarter potatoes and add to casserole. Fry for 5 minutes, then add wine and seasoning. Cover and cook over a low heat for 45 minutes.

Blanch and peel button onions. Melt remaining butter in a saucepan and fry onions till golden brown. Add to the casserole and cook for a further 10 minutes. Taste and adjust seasoning.

Serve straight from the casserole into shallow bowls at the table, accompanied by a seasonal green vegetable.

Lamb in red wine

Overall timing $2\frac{1}{2}$ hours plus overnight marination

Freezing Suitable: cook for only $1\frac{1}{2}$ hours; reheat from frozen and simmer for 30 minutes

To serve 4

2 lb	Lean lamb	900 g
1	Stalk of celery	1
1 pint	Red wine	560 ml
3	Onions	3
3 tbsp	Oil	3x15 ml
14 oz	Can of tomatoes	397 g
	Salt and pepper	

Cut the lamb into neat pieces. Trim and thinly slice the celery. Put meat and celery into a large bowl and add the wine. Cover and marinate in the refrigerator for 24 hours, turning the meat from time to time.

Peel and slice the onions. Heat the oil in a flameproof casserole and fry the onions till transparent. Drain the meat, reserving the marinade. Add the meat to the pan and fry till browned on all sides. Add the tomatoes and juice, the marinade and seasoning. Bring to the boil, then cover and simmer for about 2 hours till the meat is tender.

Taste and adjust the seasoning and serve immediately with creamed potatoes or buttered pasta.

Paprika lamb stew

Overall timing 2 hours

Freezing Suitable

To serve 6

2	Green peppers	2
2	Onions	2
1	Garlic clove	1
2 oz	Bacon rashers	50 g
2 tbsp	Oil	2x15 ml
2 lb	Boned shoulder of lamb	900 g
14 oz	Can of tomatoes	397 g
2 tbsp	Tomato purée	2x15 ml
1 teasp	Paprika	5 ml
1 teasp	Sugar	5 ml
1 pint	Stock	560 ml
	Salt and pepper	
$\frac{1}{4}$ pint	Carton of soured cream	150 ml

Deseed the peppers and cut into strips. Peel and finely chop the onions. Peel and crush the garlic. Derind and dice the bacon. Heat the oil in a flameproof casserole, add the onions, garlic and bacon and fry over a high heat till golden.

Cut the meat into cubes and add to casserole. Brown on all sides. Stir in peppers, tomatoes and their juice, tomato purée, paprika, sugar, stock and seasoning. Cover and cook gently for $1\frac{1}{2}$ hours till meat is tender.

Taste and adjust seasoning and serve with boiled potatoes and soured cream for everyone to spoon on top of the stew.

Pork

Roast pork with stuffing balls

Overall timing $2\frac{1}{4}$ hours

Freezing Not suitable

To serve 6		
$2\frac{1}{2}$ lb	Rolled boned hindloin of pork	1.1 kg
	Oil	
	Salt	
Stuffing balls		
1	Onion	1
2 oz	Butter	50 g
4 oz	Fresh breadcrumbs	125 g
2 teasp	Dried sage	2x5 ml
	Salt and pepper	
2	Eggs	2
1 oz	Lard	25 g

Preheat the oven to 450°F (230°C) Gas 8.

Score the skin on the joint, then rub it well with oil and sprinkle with salt. Place in a roasting tin and roast for 20 minutes. Reduce the temperature to 375°F (190°C) Gas 5, and continue roasting for $1\frac{1}{2}$ hours.

Meanwhile, make the stuffing balls. Peel and chop the onion. Melt the butter in a frying pan and fry the onion till golden. Tip the onion into a bowl and add the breadcrumbs, sage and seasoning. Bind with the eggs, then shape into small balls.

About 45 minutes before the pork has finished cooking, melt the lard in an oven-proof dish in the oven. Arrange the stuffing balls in the dish and place on a shelf below the pork. Turn once during the cooking.

Transfer the pork to a warmed serving platter and surround with the stuffing balls.

Kidney-stuffed roast pork

Overall timing $3\frac{1}{2}$ hours

Freezing Not suitable

To serve 4

1	Calf's kidney	1
4lb	Boned loin of pork	1.8kg
	Sprig of thyme	
	Salt and pepper	
6oz	Butter	175g
$1\frac{1}{2}$lb	Cooked potatoes	700g
3 tbsp	Oil	3x15ml
1lb	Button mushrooms	450g
1 tbsp	Chopped parsley	15ml

Preheat the oven to 375°F (190°C) Gas 5.

Prepare kidney. Spread out the pork loin and put kidney in the centre with thyme and seasoning. Roll meat tightly round kidney and tie at regular intervals with string. Place meat in roasting tin with 2oz (50g) of the butter. Roast for 3 hours, basting occasionally.

Meanwhile, slice cooked potatoes. Melt 2oz (50g) of the butter with the oil in a frying pan, add the potatoes and fry until golden.

Halve mushrooms. Melt remaining butter in another frying pan and cook the mushrooms for 5 minutes, shaking the pan from time to time.

Place meat on warmed serving plate. Surround with drained potatoes and mushrooms and garnish with chopped parsley. Serve with gravy made from roasting juices.

Braised pork with herbs

Overall timing $2\frac{3}{4}$ hours

Freezing Not suitable

To serve 6–8

3 lb	Rolled boned foreloin of pork	1.4 kg
	Salt and pepper	
6	Small onions	6
4 oz	Butter	125 g
$\frac{1}{2}$ pint	Stock	300 ml
$\frac{1}{2}$ pint	Milk	300 ml
3	Bay leaves	3
2	Sprigs of thyme	2
2	Sprigs of parsley	2
3 tbsp	Plain flour	3x15 ml
4 fl oz	Carton of single cream	113 ml
1 tbsp	Chopped parsley	15 ml

Preheat the oven to 375°F (190°C) Gas 5.

Season pork. Peel and slice onions. Melt 2 oz (50 g) of the butter in large flameproof casserole and fry onions till pale golden. Add pork and fry till browned all over. Add the stock, milk, bay leaves, thyme and parsley and bring to the boil.

Cover tightly and cook in the oven for about 2 hours till the juices run clear when the meat is pierced with a fine skewer.

Remove the pork from the casserole, put into a warmed serving dish, discard the string and keep hot. Discard the herbs from the cooking liquor.

Mix the remaining butter with the flour to make a paste and add to the pan in small amounts, stirring well between each addition. Bring to the boil, stirring constantly, and simmer till thickened. Remove from the heat, stir in cream and chopped parsley and adjust the seasoning. Pour into a warmed sauceboat and serve with the pork.

Pork with thyme and olives

Overall timing $2\frac{1}{2}$ hours

Freezing Not suitable

To serve 10

3 lb	Boned leg of pork	1.4 kg
	Sprigs of thyme	
4 oz	Stoned black olives	125 g
2 oz	Butter	50 g
1 tbsp	Oil	15 ml
	Salt and pepper	
1	Large onion	1
1	Garlic clove	1
12 oz	Ripe tomatoes	350 g
1 pint	Light stock	560 ml
1	Bay leaf	1
	Parsley stalks	
$\frac{1}{2}$ teasp	Caster sugar	2.5 ml
4 tbsp	Dry white wine	4x15 ml
4 oz	Stoned green olives	125 g

Preheat the oven to 375°F (190°C) Gas 5.

Remove skin from pork, leaving thin layer of fat over meat. Tie into a neat shape with string, then make several deep cuts through fat into meat. Push a piece of thyme and a black olive into each cut.

Heat butter and half oil in a roasting tin and brown meat all over. Season and roast for 2 hours, basting occasionally.

Meanwhile, peel and finely chop onion; peel and crush garlic. Blanch, peel and chop tomatoes. Heat remaining oil in a saucepan, add onion and fry till transparent. Add tomatoes, garlic and stock and bring to the boil. Tie remaining thyme, the bay leaf and parsley stalks together. Add to pan with sugar and seasoning and simmer for 30 minutes till thick.

Slice meat and arrange on a warmed serving dish. Pour off excess fat from tin, add wine and stir over heat to dissolve sediment. Remove herbs from sauce. Add juices from roasting tin and green olives and heat through.

Scandinavian pork

Overall timing $2\frac{1}{2}$ hours plus soaking

Freezing Not suitable

To serve 6–8

8 oz	Plump prunes	225 g
1	Large cooking apple	1
2 tbsp	Lemon juice	2x15 ml
3 lb	Piece of belly of pork	1.4 kg
	Salt and pepper	
1 tbsp	Oil	15 ml
$\frac{1}{2}$ pint	Stock	300 ml
2 tbsp	Plain flour	2x15 ml
	Sprigs of parsley	

Soak prunes in $\frac{1}{2}$ pint (300 ml) hot water for 1 hour.

Preheat the oven to 375°F (190°C) Gas 5.

Drain prunes, reserving soaking water, and remove stones. Peel, core and slice apple. Toss in lemon juice to prevent browning and add to prunes.

Season pork. Place apple and prunes along the centre, then roll up lengthways and tie into a neat shape with fine string. Place in a roasting tin and rub oil into skin. Sprinkle with salt and roast for 45 minutes.

Pour prune soaking liquor and stock over pork. Reduce the temperature to 350°F (180°C) Gas 4 and roast for a further $1\frac{1}{4}$ hours.

Place the meat on a warmed serving dish, discard the string and keep hot. Drain pan juices into a small saucepan and skim off any fat. Blend flour to a smooth paste with 4 tbsp (4x15 ml) cold water. Add to meat juices and bring to the boil, stirring constantly. Simmer for 4–5 minutes. Carve pork into thick slices and garnish with sprigs of parsley. Serve with gravy.

Roast stuffed pork roll

Overall timing $3\frac{1}{2}$ hours

Freezing Not suitable

To serve 10–12

$4\frac{1}{2}$ lb	Boned hindloin of pork	2 kg
	Piece of pork caul	
Stuffing		
2 oz	Smoked streaky bacon rashers	50 g
8 oz	Pie veal	225 g
4 oz	Pork sausagemeat	125 g
3 tbsp	Grated Parmesan cheese	3x15 ml
2 oz	Fresh breadcrumbs	50 g
1	Egg yolk	1
$\frac{1}{4}$ teasp	Grated nutmeg	1.25 ml
	Salt and pepper	

Preheat the oven to 400°F (200°C) Gas 6.

To make the stuffing, derind the bacon and mince with the veal. Add the remaining stuffing ingredients and mix well.

Remove the skin from the pork, leaving a thin layer of fat on the meat. Place fat-side down on a board and make three deep cuts along the length of the loin. Season each cut, then spoon in the stuffing, pressing it in firmly. Roll the meat into its original shape and tie at intervals with fine string. Wrap in the caul (or rub with 2 oz (50 g) butter) and secure at intervals with string. Put into a roasting tin, season and roast for $1\frac{1}{4}$ hours.

Reduce the temperature to 350°F (180°C) Gas 4 and roast for a further $1\frac{1}{2}$ hours till the juices run clear when the meat is pierced with a fine skewer. Place the pork on a warmed serving dish and remove the caul and string. Cut into thick slices and serve immediately with roast potatoes and buttered spinach.

Pork loin with milk

Overall timing $2\frac{1}{2}$ hours

Freezing Not suitable

To serve 8–10

3 lb	Boned loin of pork	1.4 kg
	Salt and pepper	
$\frac{3}{4}$ pint	Milk	400 ml
3 oz	Butter	75 g
2 tbsp	Plain flour	2x15 ml
2 teasp	Made mustard	2x5 ml
10	Small slices of bread	10

Remove skin from pork, then tie into a neat shape with fine string. Season all over and place in flameproof casserole with milk. Bring just to the boil, cover and simmer for about 2 hours till the pork is tender.

Remove casserole from heat. Lift out the meat, remove string, pat dry with kitchen paper and reserve. Strain the cooking liquor and reserve.

Melt butter in clean casserole and fry the pork till browned on all sides. Remove from pan and place on a warmed serving plate. Keep hot.

Add the flour to the casserole and stir into the butter. Cook for 1 minute, then gradually add the strained cooking liquor. Bring to the boil, stirring constantly, and simmer till thickened. Mix in the mustard and seasoning.

Lightly toast bread and spread a little of the sauce on each slice. Arrange round pork. Pour remaining sauce into a sauceboat and serve separately.

Harlequin roast

Overall timing $2\frac{1}{2}$ hours

Freezing Not suitable

To serve 4

1	Large carrot	1
3	Gherkins	3
3oz	Cooked ham	75g
$2\frac{1}{2}$ lb	Boned pork (hind loin)	1.1kg
3 tbsp	Oil	3x15ml
4 tbsp	White wine	4x15ml
1oz	Butter	25g
	Salt and pepper	

Preheat the oven to 375°F (190°C) Gas 5.

Peel carrot. Cut carrot, gherkins and ham into thick strips. Using a thin sharp knife, make holes in each end of the meat. Push carrot, gherkin and ham strips into the cuts. Tie joint into good shape with string.

Put oil and wine in roasting tin, add meat, dot with butter and season well. Place in the oven and roast for about 2 hours, basting from time to time. Serve hot or cold.

Normandy pork chops

Overall timing 55 minutes

Freezing Not suitable

To serve 4

4oz	Button onions	125g
4	Pork foreloin chops	4
	Salt and pepper	
3 tbsp	Plain flour	3x15ml
1oz	Butter	25g
2 tbsp	Oil	2x15ml
8oz	Button mushrooms	225g
4 tbsp	Calvados or brandy	4x15ml
4 tbsp	Single cream	4x15ml
1 tbsp	Chopped parsley	15ml

Blanch the onions in boiling water for 3 minutes, then drain and peel.

Trim the chops, season and coat in the flour. Melt the butter with the oil in a frying pan and fry the chops for 3 minutes on each side.

Slice the mushrooms. Add to the pan with the onions and seasoning. Cover and cook for 15–20 minutes, turning the chops once.

Pour off any fat from the pan. Warm the Calvados or brandy in a ladle, pour over the chops and set alight. When the flames die down, transfer the chops to a warmed serving dish. Keep hot.

Stir the cream into the onion mixture and cook gently for 1 minute. Pour over the chops, sprinkle with the parsley and serve with small baked apples and creamed potatoes.

Pork chops with pepper sauce

Overall timing 45 minutes

Freezing Not suitable

To serve 4

3 tbsp	Oil	3x15 ml
4	Pork chops	4
	Salt and pepper	
2 teasp	Paprika	2x5 ml
	Cayenne pepper	
1	Onion	1
1	Green pepper	1
2	Tomatoes	2
½ pint	Hot water	300 ml
2 teasp	Plain flour	2x5 ml
3 tbsp	Single cream	3x15 ml

Heat oil in frying pan. Cook chops for 10–15 minutes on each side. Season with salt, pepper, paprika and a pinch of cayenne. Place on a warmed serving dish and keep hot.

Peel and finely chop onion. Deseed and chop pepper. Blanch, peel and chop tomatoes. Cook onion in frying pan till golden. Add the pepper and water, cover and cook for 2 minutes. Add the tomatoes and cook, covered, for a further 3 minutes.

Mix flour and a little water to a smooth paste in a cup, then add to pan. Simmer, stirring, till thickened. Remove from heat and stir in the cream. Taste and adjust seasoning. Pour sauce over chops and serve.

Polish-style pork with sauerkraut

Overall timing 1 hour

Freezing Not suitable

To serve 6

3 tbsp	Oil	3x15 ml
6	Pork loin chops	6
1	Large onion	1
1	Garlic clove	1
	Salt and pepper	
2lb	Sauerkraut	900g
1	Bay leaf	1
½ pint	Chicken stock	300ml
1	Large dessert apple	1
1 teasp	Cumin seeds	5 ml

Heat the oil in flameproof casserole and fry the chops till browned on both sides. Remove from the pan and reserve.

Peel and finely chop the onion; peel and crush the garlic. Add both to the casserole and fry till transparent. Season, and add the drained sauerkraut and bay leaf. Arrange the chops on top. Pour the stock over, bring to the boil and simmer for 15 minutes.

Meanwhile, peel, core and dice the apple. Add to the pan with cumin seeds and stir well, then simmer for a further 15 minutes till the chops are tender.

Taste and adjust the seasoning. Discard the bay leaf. Serve with creamed potatoes, buttered carrots and thin slices of wholemeal bread.

Cheese-topped chops

Overall timing 50 minutes

Freezing Not suitable

To serve 6

2oz	Butter	50g
2 tbsp	Oil	2x15 ml
6	Pork loin chops	6
	Salt and pepper	
$\frac{1}{4}$ pint	Chicken stock	150ml
3	Sage leaves	3
6	Thin slices of Cheddar cheese	6
5 tbsp	Marsala	5x15 ml

Heat the butter and oil in a large frying pan and fry the chops for 5 minutes on each side till brown. Season and add the stock and chopped sage. Cover and simmer for 20 minutes.

Place a slice of cheese on each chop. Add the Marsala to the pan. Cover and cook for a further 10 minutes.

Lift the chops out on to a warmed serving plate and spoon the cooking liquor around them. Serve immediately with sauté potatoes and whole green beans or broccoli spears.

Belgian pork chops

Overall timing 40 minutes

Freezing Not suitable

To serve 4

4	Pork chops	4
	Salt and pepper	
2 tbsp	Plain flour	2x15 ml
3 tbsp	Oil	3x15 ml
4	Onions	4
$\frac{1}{4}$ pint	Beer	150 ml
$\frac{1}{4}$ pint	Chicken stock	150 ml
$1\frac{1}{2}$ lb	Brussels sprouts	700 g
1 oz	Butter	25 g
2 teasp	Cornflour	2x5 ml

Coat the chops with seasoned flour. Heat oil in frying pan and cook chops for 3 minutes on each side.

Peel and thinly slice onions. Add to pan and cook for 5 minutes. Pour in beer and stock, season and simmer for 15 minutes.

Meanwhile, trim sprouts and cook in boiling water till just tender. Drain well, toss with butter and keep hot.

Remove chops from pan and place on warmed serving plate. Surround with sprouts. Mix cornflour with a little cold water and add to pan. Bring to the boil and cook for 2 minutes. Pour sauce over chops.

Swiss pork parcels

Overall timing 50 minutes

Freezing Not suitable

To serve 6

12	Thin slices of pork fillet	12
1	Onion	1
4oz	Cooked ham	125g
4oz	Mushrooms	125g
1oz	Butter	25g
4 tbsp	Plain flour	4x15ml
4 tbsp	Lemon juice	4x15ml
1	Garlic clove	1
1	Egg yolk	1
2 tbsp	Chopped parsley	2x15ml
1 teasp	Dried rosemary	5ml
1 teasp	Dried sage	5ml
3oz	Cheese	75g
	Salt and pepper	
	Oil for frying	
2	Whole eggs	2
6 tbsp	Dried breadcrumbs	6x15ml
2	Lemons	2

Put pork slices between damp greaseproof and beat until thin. Peel and finely chop onion. Chop ham. Finely chop mushrooms. Melt butter in a saucepan and fry onion for 5 minutes. Add ham and mushrooms. Sprinkle half flour over and cook for 2 minutes. Stir in lemon juice and bring to the boil, stirring. Simmer for 3 minutes. Peel and crush garlic. Add to pan with egg yolk, herbs, grated cheese and seasoning.

Heat oil in deep-fryer to 320°F (160°C). Season remaining flour and use to coat pork slices. Spread stuffing over six slices, then cover with remaining slices and secure with wooden cocktail sticks. Beat eggs. Dip meat in eggs, then coat thickly with breadcrumbs. Fry for 5–10 minutes till golden. Drain on kitchen paper and garnish with lemon slices.

Orange pork rolls

Overall timing 1 hour

Freezing Not suitable

To serve 6

6x4oz	Slices of lean pork	6x125g
1	Onion	1
3oz	Butter	75g
4oz	Fresh breadcrumbs	125g
2 tbsp	Chopped parsley	2x15ml
1 teasp	Dried mixed herbs	5ml
	Salt and pepper	
1	Large orange	1
1	Egg	1
2 tbsp	Plain flour	2x15ml
$\frac{1}{4}$ pint	Cider	150ml
$\frac{1}{4}$ pint	Chicken stock	150ml

Preheat the oven to 375°F (190°C) Gas 5.

Place slices of pork between damp greaseproof and beat till very thin. Peel and finely chop onion. Melt 1oz (25g) of the butter in a frying pan and fry onion till golden. Add breadcrumbs, parsley, herbs and seasoning. Cook for 2 minutes, then remove from the heat.

Grate orange rind into stuffing, add egg and mix well. Divide stuffing between pork slices. Roll them up carefully, turning sides in to cover stuffing, and secure with wooden cocktail sticks.

Arrange rolls in roasting tin and dot with remaining butter. Squeeze orange and pour juice over. Cook in the oven for about 35 minutes, basting occasionally, till pork is tender.

Place pork rolls on a warmed serving dish and keep hot. Sprinkle flour into roasting tin and stir over heat for 1 minute. Gradually add cider and stock and bring to the boil, stirring. Season to taste, pour into a sauce boat and serve with the pork rolls.

Fricassee of pork

Overall timing 2 hours plus overnight marination

Freezing Not suitable

To serve 6

2lb	Lean pork	900g
6oz	Button onions	175g
4oz	Smoked streaky bacon rashers	125g
2oz	Butter	50g
2 tbsp	Plain flour	2x15ml
	Salt and pepper	
Marinade		
2	Onions	2
2	Garlic cloves	2
	Bouquet garni	
	Peppercorns	
2	Cloves	2
2–3	Sage leaves	2–3
1 tbsp	Oil	15ml
1	Bottle of red wine	1

Cut pork into 2 inch (5cm) cubes and put into a bowl. Peel and chop onions; peel and crush garlic. Add onions and garlic to meat with remaining marinade ingredients. Mix well, cover and marinate in refrigerator overnight.

The next day, lift meat out of marinade and pat dry. Blanch and peel onions. Derind bacon and cut into thin strips.

Melt butter in flameproof casserole and fry bacon and onions for 5 minutes. Remove from pan and reserve. Add pork and brown on all sides. Sprinkle in flour and cook, stirring, till it turns a rich brown colour.

Strain marinade and gradually stir into pan. Bring to the boil, stirring constantly. Return bacon and onions and season, then cover and simmer for about 1¼ hours till meat is tender.

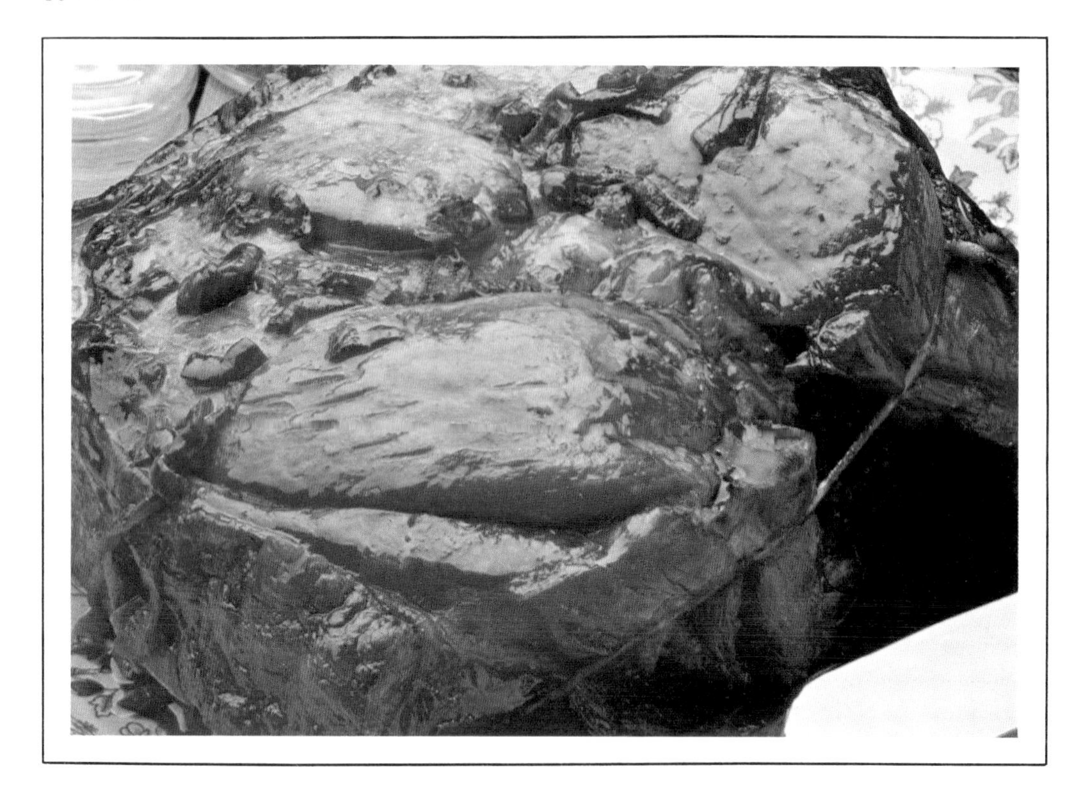

Ham roasted in stout

Overall timing $2\frac{1}{2}$ hours plus cooling

Freezing Suitable: slice meat and cover with sauce; reheat from frozen in moderate oven

To serve 6

3 lb	Lightly salted ham or bacon (collar, slipper, or gammon)	1.4 kg
2	Onions	2
$\frac{1}{2}$ pint	Stout	300 ml
1 oz	Butter	25 g
1 oz	Plain flour	25 g
$\frac{1}{4}$ teasp	Crushed caraway seed	1.25 ml
	Pepper	

Preheat the oven to 400°F (200°C) Gas 4.

If using bacon joint, remove rind. Place ham or bacon in an ovenproof dish. Peel onions and slice into rings. Cover ham with onion rings. Pour stout over. Roast for 2 hours, turning meat once during cooking.

Remove meat from dish and place on warmed serving dish. Keep hot. Sieve cooking liquor, cool quickly and skim fat from surface. Place liquor in measuring jug and make up to $\frac{1}{2}$ pint (300 ml) with water if necessary.

Melt butter in saucepan. Stir in flour and allow to brown lightly. Gradually add cooking liquor and simmer, stirring, till thickened. Season with crushed caraway seed and black pepper. Cook for 5 minutes, then pour over the roast and serve.

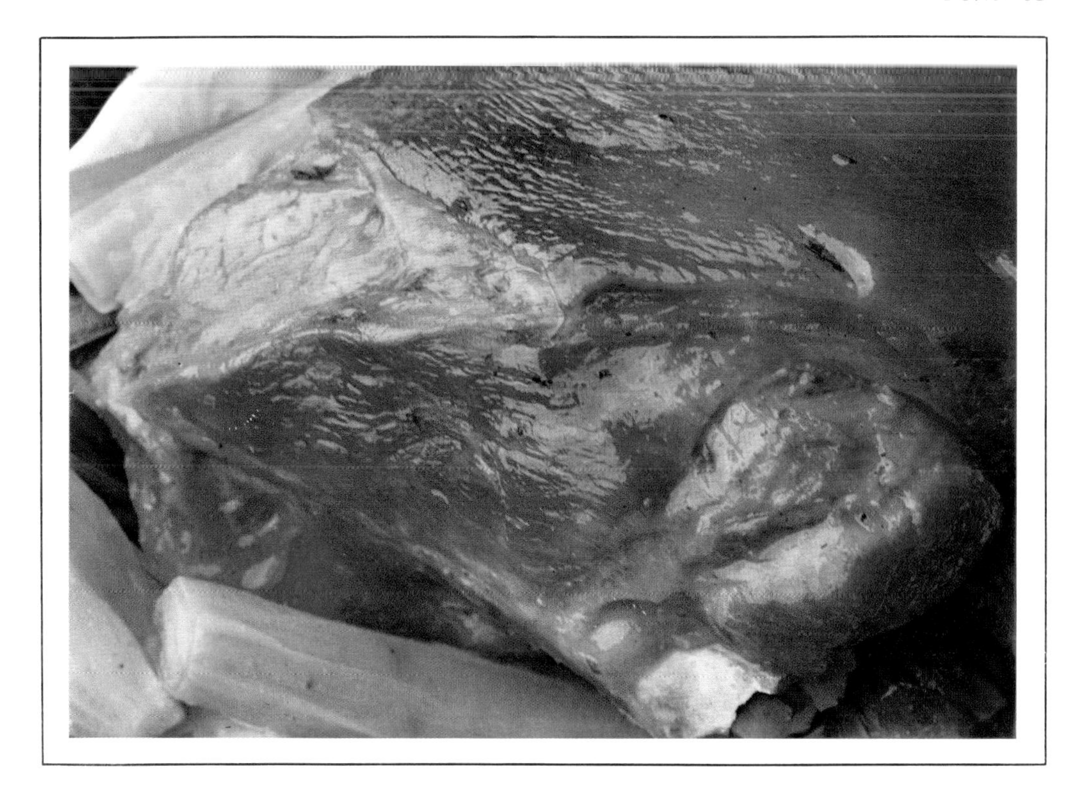

Bacon braised with leeks

Overall timing $1\frac{1}{2}$ hours

Freezing Not suitable

To serve 4–6

2 oz	Butter	50 g
2 lb	Bacon knuckle	900 g
$\frac{1}{4}$ pint	Dry white wine	150 ml
$\frac{1}{4}$ pint	Water	150 ml
	Bouquet garni	
	Salt and pepper	
2 lb	Leeks	900 g
2	Onions	2
1 teasp	Made mustard	5 ml

Melt the butter in a large flameproof casserole and brown the bacon on all sides over a high heat. Reduce heat and add wine, water, bouquet garni and seasoning. Cover and cook gently for 1 hour.

Trim leeks and cut into 3 inch (7.5 cm) lengths. Peel onions and cut into quarters. Add to casserole with seasoning and cook for a further 15–20 minutes till tender.

Remove bacon from casserole and place on warmed serving plate. Lift out vegetables with a draining spoon and arrange around joint. Keep hot. Reduce pan juices by half by rapid boiling. Stir in mustard, then spoon over vegetables. Serve immediately with new potatoes.

Italian pork kebabs

Overall timing 35 minutes

Freezing Not suitable

To serve 4		
1 lb	Pork fillet	450 g
16	Dried mushrooms	16
1 oz	Butter	25 g
2 tbsp	Cooking oil	2x15 ml
	Bay leaves	
	Salt and pepper	
4 oz	Plain flour	125 g
1	Egg	1
4 fl oz	Milk or water	120 ml
2	Egg whites	2
	Oil for deep frying	
	Lemon slices	

Cut the pork into cubes. Soak the mushrooms in water to cover for 15 minutes.

Melt the butter with 1 tbsp (15 ml) oil in a frying pan and fry the pork cubes till browned all over. Drain well. Drain the mushrooms and dry on kitchen paper. Thread the pork cubes, mushrooms and bay leaf pieces onto skewers. Season.

Sift the flour and 1½ teasp (7.5 ml) salt into a bowl. Beat in the egg, remaining oil and milk or water till smooth. Whisk the egg whites till stiff and fold into the batter.

Heat oil in a deep fryer to 320°F (160°C). Coat the kebabs in the batter and deep fry till golden. Drain on kitchen paper and serve with lemon slices.

Spaghetti with bacon sauce

Overall timing 45 minutes

Freezing Not suitable

To serve 4

12 oz	Piece of smoked streaky bacon	350 g
1 tbsp	Oil	15 ml
1	Small red pepper	1
14 oz	Can of tomatoes	397 g
	Salt and pepper	
12 oz	Spaghetti	350 g
6 tbsp	Grated Parmesan cheese	6x15 ml

Remove the rind and any bones from the bacon. Cut into $\frac{1}{4}$ inch (6 mm) thick slices, then cut across into strips. Heat the oil in a saucepan, add the bacon and fry till golden all over.

Deseed and finely chop the pepper. Add to the pan and fry for 1 minute. Press the tomatoes and juice through a sieve into the pan and bring to the boil, stirring. Add seasoning, cover and simmer for 15 minutes.

Meanwhile, cook the spaghetti in boiling salted water till tender. Drain thoroughly and return to the pan. Add the sauce and all but 1 tbsp (15 ml) of the cheese. Toss lightly over a low heat for 2 minutes. Adjust the seasoning to taste.

Place spaghetti in a warmed serving dish and sprinkle with the remaining cheese. Serve immediately with fresh crusty bread.

Sausages in cider sauce

Overall timing 50 minutes

Freezing Not suitable

To serve 4

1 lb	Boned pork chops	450 g
8	Pork chipolatas	8
1 oz	Lard	25 g
1	Large onion	1
1	Carrot	1
1	Stalk of celery	1
4	Large tomatoes	4
1	Garlic clove	1
$\frac{1}{4}$ pint	Dry cider	150 ml
	Salt and pepper	
1 oz	Butter	25 g
12 oz	Long grain rice	350 g
$1\frac{1}{2}$ pints	Chicken stock	850 ml
3 tbsp	Grated Parmesan cheese	3x15 ml

Cut the pork chops into bite size pieces. Twist each chipolata in half to make 16 small sausages. Melt the lard in a frying pan and fry the pork and sausages gently, turning frequently, for 10 minutes.

Meanwhile, peel and chop the onion and carrot. Trim and chop the celery. Quarter the tomatoes. Peel and crush the garlic. Add the vegetables to the frying pan with the cider and seasoning. Cover and simmer for 20 minutes.

Melt the butter in a saucepan, add the rice and fry, stirring, for 2 minutes. Add the stock and bring to the boil, stirring. Cover and simmer for about 15 minutes till rice is tender and liquid is absorbed.

Remove the rice from the heat and stir in the cheese. Taste and adjust the seasoning and fluff with a fork. Pile into a warmed serving dish and arrange sausages and pork on top. Spoon cider sauce over and serve immediately with a mixed salad.

Ham pie

Overall timing 1 hour

Freezing Not suitable

To serve 4

8 oz	Shortcrust pastry	225 g
1 lb	Can of ham	453 g
1	Egg	1

Preheat the oven to 425°F (220°C) Gas 7.

Roll out the dough to ¼ inch (6 mm) thickness. Place ham in centre. Dampen the dough edges and fold around the ham. Seal well. Place in ovenproof dish and decorate with trimmings, if liked.

Lightly beat the egg and brush all over the dough. Bake for 40 minutes till golden.

Savoury mould

Overall timing 2½ hours plus setting

Freezing Not suitable

To serve 8–10

2 lb	Collar bacon	900 g
1	Onion	1
1	Clove	1
1	Stalk of celery	1
2	Garlic cloves	2
	Bouquet garni	
	Salt and pepper	
5 tbsp	Chopped parsley	5x15 ml
1 tbsp	White wine vinegar	15 ml
2 teasp	Powdered gelatine	2x5 ml
1 teasp	Dried tarragon	5 ml
1 teasp	Dried chervil	5 ml
2	Egg whites	2
	Cucumber peel	
1	Red pepper	1
1 oz	Stoned black olives	25 g

Put bacon in a pan, cover with water and bring to the boil. Drain. Peel onion and spike with clove. Chop celery. Peel garlic. Add vegetables to pan with 3½ pints (2 litres) water, the bouquet garni and seasoning. Bring to the boil and simmer for 1 hour.

Soak parsley in vinegar.

Lift bacon joint out of pan. Remove meat from bone and chop. Reduce cooking liquor to ½ pint (300 ml) by boiling fast. Strain cooking liquor and return to pan. Add gelatine and herbs. Lightly beat egg whites and add. Leave for 30 minutes, then bring nearly to the boil, whisking. Remove from heat and pour through a scalded jelly bag or several layers of muslin.

Spoon a little jelly into wet pudding basin. Chill till set.

Chop cucumber peel. Deseed and slice pepper. Arrange decoratively in basin with olives. Add a little more jelly and chill again till set. Arrange bacon pieces and parsley in layers in basin. Pour remaining jelly over, cover and chill overnight.

Ham, veal and pork pie

Overall timing $2\frac{1}{2}$ hours plus overnight marination and chilling

Freezing Suitable

To serve 6–8

12 oz	Pie veal	350 g
2	Bay leaves	2
1 tbsp	Brandy	15 ml
	Salt and pepper	
8 oz	Cooked ham	225 g
12 oz	Belly of pork	350 g
4 oz	Streaky bacon	125 g
1 lb	Plain flour	450 g
5 oz	Butter	150 g
6 fl oz	Water	175 ml
2	Egg yolks	2

Cut veal into thin strips and place in a bowl with bay leaves, brandy and a pinch of salt. Leave to marinate overnight. Cut ham into thin strips, add to veal and leave to marinate for another 2 hours.

Preheat the oven to 375°F (190°C) Gas 5.

Pass pork and bacon through a mincer twice. Mix with a little of the marinade and seasoning.

Sift flour and 1 teasp (5 ml) salt into a large bowl and make a well in the centre. Melt butter in water and bring to the boil. Pour quickly into the flour and mix well. Add one egg yolk and knead to a smooth dough.

Working quickly, roll out two-thirds of dough and use to line a greased 2 lb (900 g) loaf tin. Spread half the pork mixture on bottom, cover with ham and veal mixture and spread remaining pork mixture on top. Roll out remaining dough to fit pie. Seal edges. Put strips from leftover dough on sides of rectangle, moistening first to secure.

Lightly beat remaining egg yolk with a pinch of salt and brush over dough. Bake for 1 hour, then reduce heat to 170°F (325°C) Gas 3, cover with foil to prevent over-browning and bake for another hour.

Offal

Brawn

Overall timing $3\frac{3}{4}$ hours plus brining and setting

Freezing Suitable

Makes about $3\frac{1}{2}$ lb (1.6 kg)

$\frac{1}{2}$	Pig's head	$\frac{1}{2}$
2	Pig's trotters	2
1 lb	Shin beef on bone	450 g
2	Carrots	2
2	Bouquet garni	2
4 tbsp	Lemon juice	4x15 ml
	Strips of pork fat	
Brine		
2 oz	Saltpetre	50 g
12 oz	Salt	350 g
8 oz	Brown sugar	225 g
5 pints	Water	2.8 litres
3	Cloves	3
12	Coriander seeds	12
12	Black peppercorns	12
2	Blades of mace	2

Put ingredients for brine in pan and bring to the boil, then cool. Remove brain from pig's head. Wash head and trotters thoroughly. Put into brine, put a plate on top to keep meat submerged, and leave in a cool place for 24 hours.

Drain pork and rinse. Put into clean pan. Add beef, carrots, herbs and half lemon juice, and cover with cold water. Cover and simmer for $1\frac{1}{2}$ hours till meat comes away from bones.

Lift meat out of stock and cool. Boil stock till reduced by one third. Strain into a clean pan and cool.

Cut meat from bones and dice, discarding any skin or gristle. Skim fat from stock, add meat and bring to the boil. Cover and simmer for 15 minutes.

Add remaining lemon juice. Cool, then chill till syrupy and beginning to set.

Line $3\frac{1}{2}$–4 pint (2–2.2 litre) mould with fat, add pork mixture and leave to set.

Liver pâté

Overall timing $2\frac{1}{2}$ hours plus marination and overnight chilling

Freezing Suitable

To serve 8–10		
1 lb	Pig's liver	450 g
1 lb	Streaky bacon rashers	450 g
1	Slice of bread	1
$\frac{1}{4}$ teasp	Ground allspice	1.25 ml
	Pinch of dried thyme	
1 tbsp	Brandy	15 ml
$\frac{1}{4}$ pint	Medium-dry white wine	150 ml
	Salt and pepper	
	Thin slices of pork fat	

Prepare liver. Derind the bacon. Remove crusts from bread. Mince liver, bacon and bread, then mix with allspice, thyme, brandy, wine and seasoning. Marinate in the refrigerator for 2 hours.

Preheat the oven to 400°F (200°C) Gas 6.

Line a 2 lb (900 g) loaf tin with some of the pork fat. Spread the liver mixture into the tin, press down and cover with the remaining pork fat. Cover the tin with foil and place in a roasting tin containing 1 inch (2.5 cm) of hot water. Bake for about $1\frac{3}{4}$ hours.

Remove the tin from the oven and leave to cool. Chill overnight.

Turn pâté out on to a serving dish, cut into thick slices and serve with crusty bread and a green salad.

Liver and onions

Overall timing 20 minutes

Freezing Not suitable

To serve 4

2	Large onions	2
2 oz	Butter	50 g
	Salt and pepper	
$\frac{1}{4}$ pint	Beef stock	150 ml
1 lb	Lamb's or pig's liver	450 g
3 tbsp	Plain flour	3x15 ml
$\frac{1}{4}$ pint	Wine vinegar	150 ml
1 tbsp	Chopped parsley	15 ml

Peel and slice onions. Melt half the butter in a saucepan and fry the onions till golden. Season, add stock and bring to the boil. Boil rapidly till reduced by half.

Cut liver into four slices and coat with seasoned flour. Melt the remaining butter in a frying pan and fry the liver for 2–3 minutes on each side. Arrange on a warmed serving dish and keep hot.

Pour vinegar into frying pan and boil for 1 minute. Add fried onions and stock and season to taste. Spoon mixture over liver and garnish with parsley.

Liver soufflé

Overall timing 45 minutes

Freezing Not suitable

To serve 4

12 oz	Calf's or lamb's liver	350 g
2 oz	Butter	50 g
3 tbsp	Brandy	3x15 ml
¾ pint	Thick white sauce	400 ml
	Salt and pepper	
2	Eggs	2

Preheat the oven to 400°F (200°C) Gas 6.

Cut liver into thin slices. Melt butter in a frying pan, add liver and fry for 2–3 minutes on each side. Heat the brandy in a ladle, set it alight and pour over the liver. Put liver into bender and purée.

Mix liver with white sauce and seasoning. Separate the eggs and beat the egg yolks into the liver mixture, one at a time. Whisk the egg whites till stiff but not dry and fold into the liver mixture with a metal spoon.

Pour mixture into a greased 8 inch (20 cm) soufflé dish, smooth top and bake for about 25 minutes till well risen and golden. Serve immediately with a crisp green salad.

Chicken livers with Marsala

Overall timing 15 minutes

Freezing Not suitable

To serve 6

3oz	Butter	75g
1lb	Chicken livers	450g
4	Sage leaves	4
	Salt and pepper	
4 tbsp	Marsala	4x15 ml

Melt half the butter in a frying pan, add the livers and sage leaves and cook for 5 minutes on a high heat, turning the mixture over constantly with a wooden spoon. Season and cook for a further 1 minute.

Remove the livers from pan with a draining spoon and keep warm in a serving dish. Add Marsala to pan juices and cook for 1 minute, then add remaining butter. Continue simmering, stirring all the time, till the sauce thickens slightly. Pour sauce over liver and serve immediately with a green vegetable and sauté potatoes.

A little cream may be added to the sauce instead of the remainder of the butter if you prefer a creamier mixture.

Sweetbreads in sherry

Overall timing 30 minutes

Freezing Not suitable

To serve 4

1 lb	Prepared calves' sweetbreads	450 g
	Salt and pepper	
4 tbsp	Plain flour	4x15 ml
3 oz	Butter	75 g
5 tbsp	Sherry	5x15 ml
14 oz	Can of beef consommé	397 g
4 tbsp	Oil	4x15 ml
4	Slices of French bread	4
	Sprigs of parsley	

Cut the sweetbreads lengthways into thick slices and coat with seasoned flour. Melt 2 oz (50 g) of the butter in a frying pan, add the sweetbreads and fry over a high heat till golden on both sides.

Add the sherry and cook over a high heat till evaporated. Add the consommé, cover and simmer for 15 minutes.

Meanwhile, melt the remaining butter with the oil in another frying pan. Add the bread and fry till crisp and golden. Drain on kitchen paper, arrange on a warmed serving dish and keep hot.

Taste the sweetbreads and adjust the seasoning. Arrange on the fried bread, garnish with parsley and serve immediately with minted peas.

Kidneys with mustard sauce

Overall timing 25 minutes

Freezing Not suitable

To serve 4

1 lb	Lamb's kidneys	450 g
8 oz	Pork chipolatas	225 g
2 oz	Butter	50 g
4 oz	Button mushrooms	125 g
2	Blades of mace	2
	Salt and pepper	
¼ pint	Dry white wine	150 ml
1 tbsp	Made English mustard	15 ml

Prepare and quarter kidneys. Twist chipolatas in half to make 16 small sausages. Melt half the butter in frying pan and cook chipolatas for about 10 minutes till brown all over. Remove from pan and keep hot.

Add remaining butter to the pan with mushrooms, crushed mace and kidneys and fry for 10 minutes, stirring occasionally. Season. Remove from pan, arrange on a warmed serving dish with chipolatas and keep hot.

Pour wine into frying pan and cook, stirring, for 2–3 minutes. Remove from heat and stir in the mustard. Pour sauce over kidney mixture. Garnish with croûtons and serve with boiled rice.

Braised tongue and onions

Overall timing 4 hours

Freezing Not suitable

To serve 8–10

4 lb	Ox tongue	1.8 kg
2 lb	Onions	900 g
1	Carrot	1
1	Stalk of celery	1
	Bouquet garni	
2 tbsp	Lemon juice	2x15 ml
12 oz	Firm ripe tomatoes	350 g
2	Garlic cloves	2
2 oz	Butter	50 g
$\frac{1}{4}$ pint	Red wine	150 ml
$\frac{3}{4}$ pint	Beef stock	400 ml
	Salt and pepper	
1 tbsp	Chopped parsley	15 ml

Put tongue into a large saucepan. Peel one onion and the carrot. Add to pan with celery, bouquet garni and lemon juice and cover with cold water. Bring to the boil, cover and simmer for 2 hours till tender. Remove from the heat and leave tongue to cool in liquor.

Meanwhile, peel and slice remaining onions. Blanch, peel and quarter tomatoes. Peel and crush garlic. Preheat the oven to 400°F (200°C) Gas 6.

Melt butter in a flameproof casserole and fry onions till golden. Add wine and boil rapidly till reduced by half. Stir in garlic, stock, tomatoes and seasoning. Drain tongue, then remove skin and any small bones. Add tongue to casserole and baste with liquor. Cover tightly and bake for 1 hour till tongue is tender when pierced with a knife.

Lift tongue out of liquor and slice thickly. Arrange on a serving dish and keep hot. Add parsley to liquor and adjust seasoning. Spoon sauce over tongue and serve.

Braised stuffed hearts

Overall timing 2 hours

Freezing Not suitable

To serve 6–8

1	Onion	1
2 oz	Butter	50 g
4 oz	Long-grain rice	125 g
¾ pint	Stock	400 ml
2	Calves' hearts *or*	2
4	Lambs' hearts	4
1	Lemon	1
2 tbsp	Chopped parsley	2x15 ml
1 tbsp	Chopped fresh sage	15 ml
1	Egg	1
	Salt and pepper	
8 oz	Streaky bacon rashers	225 g
2 tbsp	Dry sherry	2x15 ml

Preheat the oven to 350°F (180°C) Gas 4.

Peel and chop onion. Melt half the butter in a pan and fry onion till golden. Add rice and ½ pint (300 ml) of the stock. Bring to the boil, cover and simmer for 20 minutes till tender. Remove from the heat.

Prepare hearts, using kitchen scissors to cut through pockets inside. Wash well and dry with kitchen paper. Grate rind and squeeze juice from lemon. Add both to pan with parsley, sage, egg and seasoning. Mix well and spoon into hearts.

Derind bacon rashers and stretch with the back of a knife. Wrap around the hearts, tying them on with fine string.

Melt remaining butter in flameproof casserole and brown hearts all over. Pour over remaining stock, add sherry, cover and cook in the oven for 1 hour.

Remove string and slice hearts. Arrange on serving dish, garnish with sage and serve.

Brains Milan-style

Overall timing 15 minutes plus soaking and cooling

Freezing Not suitable

To serve 4

4	Lambs' brains	4
2 teasp	Vinegar	2x5 ml
	Salt and pepper	
	Bouquet garni	
4 tbsp	Plain flour	4x15 ml
1	Egg	1
4 tbsp	Fresh breadcrumbs	4x15 ml
2 oz	Butter	50 g
	Sage leaves	
	Lemon wedges	

Put the brains in a bowl of cold water with 1 teasp (5 ml) of the vinegar. Soak for 15 minutes.

Drain the brains. Holding them under running water, carefully pull away membranes and blood vessels. Put the brains into a saucepan and cover with cold water. Add the remaining vinegar, salt and bouquet garni. Bring to the boil, then remove from the heat. Leave to cool in the liquid.

Drain the brains and dry on kitchen paper. Break into small pieces and coat with the flour. Beat the egg. Dip the brains into the egg, then coat with the breadcrumbs.

Melt the butter in a frying pan till foaming. Add the brains and cook for 5 minutes till brown on all sides. Garnish with sage leaves and serve with lemon wedges.

Tripe with garlic and parsley

Overall timing $2\frac{1}{2}$ hours

Freezing Not suitable

To serve 4

1	Large onion	1
1	Large carrot	1
2	Stalks of celery	2
6	Peppercorns	6
	Bay leaf	
3 pints	Cold water	1.7 litres
1 tbsp	Lemon juice	15 ml
$1\frac{1}{2}$ lb	Dressed tripe	700 g
	Salt and pepper	
4 tbsp	Plain flour	4x15 ml
2 oz	Butter	50 g
4 tbsp	Oil	4x15 ml
2–3	Garlic cloves	2–3
	Bunch of parsley	

Peel and chop the onion and carrot. Chop the celery. Put the vegetables in a saucepan with the peppercorns, bay leaf, water and lemon juice. Bring to the boil, half cover and simmer for 30 minutes. Strain and return to the pan.

Cut the tripe into pieces. Add to the pan and bring to the boil. Skim off any scum, then cover and simmer for $1\frac{1}{2}$–2 hours till tender. Test occasionally with the point of a knife.

Drain the tripe, discarding the stock, and cut into strips about $\frac{1}{2}$ inch (12.5 mm) wide. Coat with seasoned flour. Heat the butter and oil in a frying pan, add the tripe and fry over a moderate heat for 10 minutes, stirring occasionally, till golden.

Peel the garlic and chop with parsley. Sprinkle over the tripe with seasoning and place in a warmed serving dish.

Breaded trotters

Overall timing 3 hours

Freezing Not suitable

To serve 4

2	Pig's trotters	2
	Salt and pepper	
2	Onions	2
4	Cloves	4
2	Carrots	2
1	Stalk of celery	1
	Bouquet garni	
12	Peppercorns	12
1	Egg	1
1 oz	Dried breadcrumbs	25 g
	Watercress	

Remove any hairs from trotters by singeing or plucking. Scrub well and rub with salt. Wash and pat dry, then blanch in boiling salted water for 5 minutes.

Meanwhile, peel the onions and stud with the cloves. Peel the carrots. Drain the trotters and return to the pan. Add the onions, carrots, celery, bouquet garni and peppercorns. Cover with cold water. Bring to the boil and simmer for about $2\frac{1}{2}$ hours till tender. Drain and cool.

Preheat the grill.

Split the trotters lengthways. Beat the egg. Dip the trotters in the egg, then coat in the breadcrumbs.

Grill the trotters for about 10 minutes, turning occasionally, till crisp and golden. Garnish with watercress and serve with sauté potatoes and mustard.

Kidney brochettes

Overall timing 25 minutes

Freezing Not suitable

To serve 4

4oz	Unsalted butter	125g
2 tbsp	Chopped parsley	2x15ml
1 tbsp	Lemon juice	15ml
1lb	Lambs' kidneys	450g
3	Tomatoes	3
1 teasp	Dried rosemary	5ml
2 tbsp	Oil	2x15ml
	Salt and pepper	

Mash the butter with the parsley and lemon juice until well combined. Form into a roll, wrap in greaseproof paper and chill until firm.

Preheat the grill.

Prepare kidneys and cut in half. Cut tomatoes into thin wedges. Thread kidneys and tomato wedges alternately on skewers. Sprinkle with rosemary and brush with oil.

Grill for 10–15 minutes, turning once. Season and garnish with pats of parsley butter. Serve immediately with matchstick chips and sprigs of watercress.

Swiss liver kebabs

Overall timing 35 minutes

Freezing Not suitable

To serve 4

1lb	Calf's or lamb's liver	450g
	Salt and pepper	
10	Sage leaves	10
10	Streaky bacon rashers	10
2oz	Butter	50g

Preheat the grill.

Cut the liver into 20 bite-size lengths. Season. Wash and dry sage leaves. Derind and stretch the bacon rashers, then cut in half. Wrap bacon rashers round liver pieces, including a sage leaf in alternate rolls. Thread on to four oiled skewers.

Melt the butter in the bottom of the grill pan. Balance the skewers across the pan and brush butter over. Grill for 10–15 minutes till cooked and crisp, turning frequently and brushing with butter. Serve immediately with boiled new potatoes.

Liver pâté in aspic

Overall timing 2 hours plus setting

Freezing Suitable: add aspic after thawing

To serve 8–10

1 lb	Pig's liver	450 g
1 lb	Streaky bacon	450 g
1	Slice of bread	1
6 oz	Lard	175 g
3 oz	Plain flour	75 g
2 tbsp	Chopped parsley	2x15 ml
1 teasp	Dried mixed herbs	5 ml
	Salt and pepper	
1	Onion	1
3	Eggs	3
$\frac{3}{4}$ pint	Liquid aspic	400 ml
2 tbsp	Marsala	2x15 ml

Preheat the oven to 350°F (180°C) Gas 4.

Mince liver, bacon and bread. Melt lard. Mix all but 1 tbsp (15 ml) into meat with flour, herbs and seasoning. Peel and finely chop onion. Fry in remaining lard till golden. Add to mixture with eggs. Spoon into greased 2 pint (1.1 litre) mould, and cover with foil. Place in tin containing hot water and cook in oven for $1\frac{1}{2}$ hours. Cool, turn out on to a plate and chill. Chill mould.

Flavour aspic with Marsala. Use one-third to line mould. Chill till set. Return pâté to mould; pour remaining aspic down sides. Chill till set.

Terrine with port

Overall timing $1\frac{1}{2}$ hours plus 12 hours marination and 12 hours refrigeration

Freezing Suitable

To serve 6

4 fl oz	Port	120 ml
1 teasp	Dried thyme	5 ml
2	Bay leaves	2
$\frac{1}{2}$ teasp	Grated nutmeg	2.5 ml
	Salt and pepper	
1 tbsp	Oil	15 ml
12 oz	Chicken livers	350 g
4 oz	Belly of pork	125 g
4 oz	Pie veal	125 g
7 oz	Streaky bacon	200 g

Mix port, thyme, one bay leaf, nutmeg, pepper and oil. Add chicken livers, and marinate in refrigerator overnight.

The next day, mince pork and veal. Remove livers from marinade; chop four and mince rest. Mix minced meats, strained marinade and salt.

Preheat the oven to 350°F (180°C) Gas 4.

Line terrine with two-thirds of bacon. Spread half mince in dish. Cover with chopped livers and top with remaining mince. Press down well. Place remaining bay leaf on top. Cover with rest of bacon, then with foil.

Put dish in tin containing hot water. Cook in oven for about 1 hour. Cool, then chill overnight before serving.

Roast chicken with tarragon

Overall timing $1\frac{1}{4}$ hours

Freezing Suitable: pack gravy separately; serve cold

To serve 4

$3\frac{1}{2}$ lb	Ovenready chicken	1.6kg
	Salt and pepper	
2oz	Butter	50g
4 tbsp	Chopped fresh tarragon	4x15ml
	Wine, water or chicken stock	
	Watercress	

Preheat the oven to 425°F (220°C) Gas 7.

Season chicken inside and out. Put 1oz (25g) of the butter and the tarragon inside bird. Place chicken on its side in a roasting tin and coat with remaining butter. Roast for 15 minutes, then turn the chicken on to its other side. Roast for 15 minutes, then turn chicken on its back and continue roasting for 35 minutes.

Remove chicken from roasting tin and place on a warmed serving dish. Stir a little wine, water or chicken stock into the juices in the tin, bring to the boil and cook for 1 minute. Pour gravy into gravy boat. Garnish chicken with watercress.

Chicken and pepper sauté

Overall timing 1 hour

Freezing Not suitable

To serve 6

$3\frac{1}{2}$ lb	Ovenready chicken	1.6 kg
2 oz	Butter	50 g
2 tbsp	Oil	2x15 ml
12 oz	Large ripe tomatoes	350 g
	Salt and pepper	
2	Large red peppers	2
2	Large yellow peppers	2
1	Small onion	1
$\frac{1}{4}$ pint	Dry white wine	150 ml
$\frac{1}{4}$ pint	Chicken stock	150 ml

Cut chicken into six portions. Heat the butter and oil in frying pan. Add chicken pieces and brown on all sides. Blanch, peel and quarter the tomatoes. Add to the pan with plenty of seasoning. Cover and cook over a low heat for 15 minutes.

Meanwhile, preheat the grill. Place the peppers on the grill pan (cut them in half lengthways if too large to fit under) and grill, turning frequently, till the skin blisters. Remove from the grill, and peel away the charred skin. Discard the pith and seeds and cut flesh into large chunks. Add to the chicken, cover and cook for a further 10 minutes.

Peel and finely chop the onion. Remove chicken and peppers from pan and keep hot. Pour off all but 2 tbsp (2x15 ml) of the fat from the pan. Add the onion and fry till transparent. Add the wine and stock, stirring to deglaze the pan, and bring to the boil. Boil rapidly till reduced to about 6 tbsp (6x15 ml), then taste and adjust the seasoning. Return the chicken and peppers to the pan and turn till lightly coated with the liquor. Serve with plain boiled rice and a tossed green salad.

Tunisian chicken

Overall timing $2\frac{1}{4}$ hours

Freezing Not suitable

To serve 4

3 lb	Ovenready chicken with giblets	1.4 kg
	Salt and pepper	
5 oz	Sweetcorn kernels	150 g
3	Carrots	3
3	Medium potatoes	3
4	Tomatoes	4
4 oz	Cheddar cheese	125 g
1	Egg	1
2 tbsp	Breadcrumbs	2x15 ml
1	Hard-boiled egg	1
1	Stalk of celery	1
1	Sprig of parsley	1
2 oz	Butter	50 g
4 tbsp	Oil	4x15 ml

Season chicken inside and out. Chop heart, liver and gizzard. Drain sweetcorn. Peel carrots and potatoes. Blanch, peel and quarter tomatoes.

Dice the cheese and mix with the sweetcorn, giblets, egg and breadcrumbs. Mash the hard-boiled egg with a fork and add to the mixture with seasoning. Mix well. Stuff the chicken with the mixture, then close opening.

Put carrots, potatoes and tomatoes into a flameproof casserole with celery and parsley. Cover with $2\frac{1}{2}$ pints (1.5 litres) water and bring to the boil. Lower heat and add chicken with half the butter. Cover and simmer for $1\frac{1}{2}$ hours.

Remove chicken and drain on kitchen paper. Strain cooking liquor and return to casserole. Purée vegetables and add to casserole. Heat soup through.

Heat remaining butter and oil in a frying pan. Put in whole chicken and brown evenly, turning it over with two spoons. Bring chicken and soup to table in separate dishes.

Roast ginger chicken

Overall timing $1\frac{1}{4}$ hours

Freezing Not suitable

To serve 4

1	Cooking apple	1
1 inch	Piece of root ginger	2.5 cm
4 oz	Cooked long grain rice	125 g
5 oz	Carton of natural yogurt	141 g
3 oz	Softened butter	75 g
	Salt and pepper	
3 lb	Ovenready chicken	1.4 kg

Preheat the oven to 400°F (200°C) Gas 6.

Peel, core and grate apple. Grate or finely chop ginger and add to apple with rice, yogurt, 2 oz (50 g) of the butter and seasoning. Mix well together. Use to stuff chicken.

Place chicken on its side in a roasting tin and dot with remaining butter. Roast for 15 minutes, then turn chicken on to its other side and roast for 15 minutes. Turn chicken on to its back and continue roasting for a further 30 minutes or until tender. Baste frequently.

Remove chicken from roasting tin and place on warmed serving dish. Serve with gravy made from pan juices, green or mixed salad and sauté or creamed potatoes.

Portuguese-style capon

Overall timing 3 hours plus marination

Freezing Not suitable

To serve 6

$4\frac{1}{2}$ lb	Ovenready capon with giblets	2kg
	Salt and pepper	
1 pint	Dry white wine	560ml
2	Medium onions	2
4oz	Butter	125g
$\frac{1}{4}$ teasp	Grated nutmeg	1.25ml
$\frac{1}{4}$ teasp	Ground cinnamon	1.25ml
4oz	Stoned green olives	125g
2	Hard-boiled eggs	2
1oz	Stale bread	25g
3fl oz	Milk	90ml
1 teasp	Vinegar	15ml
$1\frac{1}{2}$ lb	Potatoes	700g

Season capon inside and out and put in a deep pot. Pour wine over capon, cover and marinate for a few hours in refrigerator, turning from time to time.

Cook heart in boiling water for 10 minutes. Add liver and cook for a further 10 minutes. Drain and finely chop.

Preheat the oven to 400°F (200°C) Gas 6.

Peel and finely chop onions. Melt 3oz (75g) butter and fry onions till light brown. Remove from heat and add nutmeg, cinnamon and seasoning. Finely chop green olives and hard-boiled eggs and add to stuffing with crumbled bread, milk, vinegar and heart and liver.

Fill capon with stuffing. Grease roasting tin with half remaining butter and place capon in it, reserving marinade. Rub remaining butter over capon. Half fill roasting tin with marinade. Cook in oven for $1\frac{1}{2}$–2 hours, basting occasionally. Peel and chop potatoes and roast in separate tin.

Lift capon on to warmed serving dish and surround with potatoes. Pour any remaining marinade into roasting tin and reduce over high heat. Strain into sauce boat.

Garlic chicken

Overall timing $1\frac{3}{4}$ hours

Freezing Not suitable

To serve 4

2oz	Butter	50g
1 tbsp	Oil	15ml
8	Chicken legs and wings	8
	Salt and pepper	
1	Whole garlic bulb	1
$\frac{1}{4}$ pint	Dry white wine	150ml
$\frac{3}{4}$ pint	Hot milk	400ml
1 teasp	Cornflour	5ml
2 tbsp	Single cream	2x15ml
$\frac{1}{4}$ teasp	Cayenne pepper	1.25ml

Heat half the butter and the oil in a flameproof casserole. Add the chicken and brown on all sides. Season and cook for 10–15 minutes over a low heat. Remove chicken from pan and keep warm.

Peel and crush all the garlic cloves. Add remaining butter to casserole with garlic and cook over a low heat, stirring with a wooden spoon, till soft.

Add the wine, bring to the boil and simmer for 3 minutes. Replace chicken in casserole and pour in hot milk. Cover and simmer for 20–30 minutes.

Blend the cornflour and cream in a bowl. Stir in 3 tbsp (3x15ml) of cooking liquor from casserole and add cayenne pepper. Stir cream mixture into casserole and simmer for 2–3 minutes.

Put chicken pieces into a warmed serving dish and spoon sauce over. Serve with green beans and mashed potatoes.

Chicken Maryland

Overall timing $1\frac{3}{4}$ hours

Freezing Not suitable

To serve 8

8	Boned chicken breasts	8
	Salt	
	Cayenne pepper	
2oz	Plain flour	50g
2	Eggs	2
4oz	Fresh breadcrumbs	125g
	Oil for frying	
4	Bananas	4
12	Bacon rashers	12
Corn fritters		
4oz	Plain flour	125g
1	Whole egg	1
$\frac{1}{4}$ pint	Milk	150ml
$11\frac{1}{2}$oz	Sweetcorn kernels	325g
1	Egg white	1

To make the fritter batter, sift flour and pinch of salt into a bowl and make a well in the centre. Add the whole egg and gradually beat in the milk. Drain corn and add. Leave batter to stand.

Cut each chicken breast in half. Season with salt and cayenne pepper. Dip into the flour, then into beaten eggs, then into breadcrumbs.

Heat the oil in a deep-fryer until hot enough to brown a cube of bread in 30 seconds. Fry the chicken pieces a few at a time for about 10–15 minutes, depending on thickness. Remove from pan, drain on kitchen paper and keep hot. Skim surface of oil.

Peel bananas and cut into three, then halve each piece lengthways. Derind and stretch bacon rashers and cut in half. Wrap a piece of bacon round each piece of banana and secure with a wooden cocktail stick. Fry in hot oil, then drain and keep hot.

Whisk egg white till stiff and fold into fritter batter. Drop in spoonfuls into hot oil and fry till puffed and golden brown. Drain. Arrange fritters, chicken and bacon-wrapped bananas on plate and serve.

Chicken with wine and mushroom sauce

Overall timing 1½ hours

Freezing Suitable: reheat in 350°F (180°C) Gas 4 oven for 45 minutes

To serve 4–6

3 lb	Ovenready chicken	1.4 kg
	Salt and pepper	
3½ oz	Butter	90 g
8 oz	Button mushrooms	225 g
1½ oz	Plain flour	40 g
½ pint	Dry white wine	300 ml
½ pint	Chicken stock	300 ml
1	Egg yolk	1
1 tbsp	Lemon juice	15 ml

Preheat the oven to 400°F (200°C) Gas 6.

Rub chicken with salt and dot with 1 oz (25 g) butter. Place in a roasting tin and roast for 1¼ hours, basting occasionally.

Meanwhile, thinly slice mushrooms. Melt 1 oz (25 g) butter in a frying pan, add mushrooms, sprinkle with salt and fry for 2 minutes. Remove from heat.

Melt remaining butter in a saucepan, stir in flour and cook for 1 minute. Gradually add wine and stock. Bring to the boil, stirring, and simmer till thickened. Add drained mushrooms, beaten egg yolk, lemon juice and seasoning. Return to gentle heat and cook, stirring, till sauce is smooth and of coating consistency. Place in larger pan of simmering water to keep hot.

Remove chicken from oven and cut into portions, removing skin if liked. Place in warmed serving dish, cover with the sauce and serve immediately with roast potatoes and broccoli spears.

Chicken pieces with nutty sauce

Overall timing 1 hour plus marination

Freezing Not suitable

To serve 4

5	Onions	5
1	Garlic clove	1
2oz	Walnuts	50g
	Salt	
3 tbsp	Lemon juice	3x15ml
4	Boned chicken breasts	4
2 tbsp	Groundnut oil	2x15ml
	Pinch of chilli powder	
2oz	Roasted peanuts	50g
2 teasp	Soy sauce	2x5ml
$\frac{1}{2}$ pint	Water	300ml

Peel and finely chop two onions. Peel and crush garlic. Place both in a mortar or blender with walnuts and salt. Crush or blend to a paste, gradually adding 2 tbsp (2x15ml) lemon juice to give a creamy mixture. Cut chicken into bite-size pieces. Place in a shallow dish and pour walnut mixture over. Leave to marinate for 1 hour, turning occasionally.

Meanwhile, peel and finely chop two onions. Heat half oil in a frying pan and fry onions till crisp and golden. Remove from pan and drain. Preheat the grill.

Peel and finely chop remaining onion and purée in mortar or blender with chilli powder, salt and peanuts till smooth. Heat remaining oil in pan and fry peanut mixture for 3 minutes, stirring constantly. Stir in soy sauce, water and remaining lemon juice. Cook over low heat for 5 minutes.

Thread chicken pieces on to four oiled skewers. Grill for 10 minutes, turning frequently and brushing with walnut mixture. Add any remaining walnut mixture and fried onions to peanut sauce and heat through.

Poached chicken

Overall timing 2 hours

Freezing Not suitable

To serve 4

8	Chicken legs and wings	8
12oz	Carrots	350g
8oz	Button onions	225g
2	Stalks of celery	2
	Salt	
1lb	Potatoes	450g

Put chicken joints in a large saucepan and cover with cold water. Peel and chop carrots; peel onions; chop celery. Add a few pieces of carrot, four onions, all the celery and salt to chicken. Bring slowly to the boil, then reduce the heat until just simmering, cover and cook for about $1\frac{1}{2}$ hours.

Meanwhile, cook remaining carrots and onions in boiling salted water for 5 minutes. Peel and chop potatoes and add to pan. Simmer for a further 20 minutes. Drain and keep hot.

Drain chicken (keep the cooking liquor and vegetables for soup) and serve on a warmed plate with the separately cooked carrots, onions and potatoes.

Creole chicken

Overall timing $1\frac{1}{4}$ hours

Freezing Not suitable

To serve 4

3oz	Butter	75g
1	Garlic clove	1
4oz	Dried breadcrumbs	125g
1	Sugar lump	1
2	Limes	2
5 tbsp	Rum	5x15ml
	Grated nutmeg	
	Cayenne pepper	
	Salt and pepper	
5	Bananas	5
2oz	Mixed nuts	50g
1 tbsp	Desiccated coconut	15ml
3lb	Ovenready chicken	1.4kg
9fl oz	Chicken stock	250ml

Preheat the oven to 425°F (220°C) Gas 7.

Melt 2oz (50g) butter in a pan and brown peeled and lightly bruised garlic clove. Remove from pan and discard. Fry breadcrumbs till brown.

Rub sugar lump over rind of limes to absorb zest. Crush and add to pan. Squeeze limes and add 3 tbsp (3x15ml) juice to the pan with 1 tbsp (15ml) of rum, a pinch each of nutmeg and cayenne and seasoning. Stir for a few minutes, then remove from the heat and leave till breadcrumbs absorb liquid.

Peel and mash bananas. Mix in chopped nuts, coconut, remaining lime juice, 1 tbsp (15ml) of rum and seasoning.

Stuff breadcrumb mixture into one end of chicken and banana mixture into the other. Close both ends. Place in roasting tin and dot with remaining butter. Roast for 1 hour.

Remove chicken from tin, place on serving plate and keep warm. Pour chicken stock into tin and mix with pan juices. Bring to the boil and simmer for 2–3 minutes. Warm remaining rum, set alight and pour over the chicken. Serve with gravy and fried bananas.

Chicken pie

Overall timing $1\frac{1}{2}$ hours

Freezing Suitable: reheat, covered, in 350°F (180°C) Gas 4 oven for 40 minutes

To serve 6

$7\frac{1}{2}$ oz	Frozen puff pastry	212 g
2	Onions	2
8 fl oz	Dry white wine	220 ml
$2\frac{1}{2}$ lb	Chicken joints	1.1 kg
	Salt and pepper	
8 oz	Streaky bacon rashers	225 g
2 oz	Butter	50 g
8 fl oz	Hot chicken stock	220 ml
8 oz	Button mushrooms	225 g
2 tbsp	Chopped parsley	2x15 ml
1 teasp	Arrowroot	5 ml
1	Egg yolk	1

Preheat the oven to 425°F (220°C) Gas 7.

Thaw pastry. Peel and chop one onion and cook in wine for 5 minutes. Remove chicken meat from bones and season. Derind bacon rashers.

Melt butter in a pan. Add chicken and fry for a few minutes, then add onion and wine and hot stock. Cook gently for 20 minutes.

Line ovenproof dish with half the bacon rashers. Remove chicken from pan with a draining spoon and place in dish. Peel and chop remaining onion. Slice mushrooms. Sprinkle onion, parsley and mushrooms over chicken. Place remaining bacon rashers over top. Stir arrowroot into cooking liquor in pan, then pour into dish.

Dampen edges of dish, then roll out dough and cover dish. Decorate with trimmings. Brush with beaten egg yolk. Bake for 15 minutes. Reduce heat to 400°F (200°C) Gas 6, and bake for a further 30 minutes.

Normandy duck

Overall timing 1 hour 10 minutes

Freezing Not suitable

To serve 4

	Sprigs of tarragon	
4½ lb	Ovenready duck	2kg
3oz	Butter	75g
2 tbsp	Calvados or brandy	2x15ml
	Salt and pepper	
4	Granny Smith apples	4
¼ pint	Dry white wine	150ml
½ pint	Carton of single cream	284ml

Chop tarragon and set some aside for sauce. Place the rest inside the duck. Prick the skin all over with a fork.

Melt 2oz (50g) butter in a large flameproof casserole. Add the duck and brown on all sides. Warm the Calvados or brandy in a ladle, pour it over the duck and set alight. When the flames die down, season, cover and simmer for 45 minutes, turning the bird over halfway through.

Peel and core apples and cut into thick slices. Melt remaining butter in a frying pan and fry apples till brown.

Remove duck from casserole and keep warm. Skim fat off cooking juices, then add wine. Reduce by boiling fast for a few minutes. Add cream and reserve chopped tarragon. Stir over gentle heat for a few minutes.

Place duck on a warmed serving dish, surround with apple slices and serve sauce separately.

Roast duck with turnips

Overall timing 2 hours

Freezing Not suitable

To serve 4

4 lb	Ovenready duck with giblets	1.8 kg
1	Onion	1
1	Carrot	1
$2\frac{1}{2}$ oz	Butter	65 g
	Bouquet garni	
$\frac{1}{4}$ pint	Dry cider	150 ml
$\frac{1}{4}$ pint	Water	150 ml
	Salt and pepper	
4 tbsp	Honey	4x15 ml
2 lb	Small turnips	900 g
1 tbsp	Caster sugar	15 ml
8 oz	Button onions	225 g

Preheat the oven to 400°F (200°C) Gas 6.

Season duck inside and out. Place on a wire rack in roasting tin. Prick all over with a fork. Roast for 45 minutes.

Meanwhile, peel and chop onion. Peel and slice carrot. Melt $\frac{1}{2}$ oz (15 g) of the butter in a frying pan and fry giblets and onions for a few minutes. Add carrot, bouquet garni, cider, water and seasoning. Simmer for 30 minutes. Strain and stir in honey.

Peel turnips. Melt remaining butter in the frying pan, add turnips and sprinkle with sugar. Brown turnips on all sides. Peel button onions and add to turnips. Cook for a further 5 minutes.

Reduce oven temperature to 350°F (180°C) Gas 4. Drain off excess fat from roasting tin and pour in honey mixture. Arrange turnips and onions around duck and roast for a further 45 minutes, basting frequently.

Place duck on a warmed serving plate, surround by the vegetables and spoon over any hot glaze left in roasting tin.

Index